THE DOCTRINE OF THE LAITY

THE DOCTRINE OF THE LAITY

FINDLEY B. EDGE

Convention Press • Nashville, Tennessee

Convention Press
Nashville, Tennessee

© Copyright 1985 • Convention Press
All rights reserved

5133-95

This book is the text for course 05045
in the subject area Baptist Doctrine
in the Church Study Course

Dewey Decimal Classification: 253
Subject Heading: LAITY

Printed in the United States of America

Adult Section
Church Training Department
The Sunday School Board of the Southern Baptist Convention
127 Ninth Avenue, North
Nashville, Tennessee 37234

Acknowledgements

Unless stated otherwise, the Scripture verses quoted in this book are from the King James Version.

Quotations marked Beck are from *The Holy Bible in the Language of Today* by William F. Beck. Copyright © Mrs. William F. Beck, 1976. Published by Holman Bible Publishers. Used by permission.

Quotations marked GNB are from the *Good News Bible,* the Bible in Today's English Version. Old Testament: Copyright © American Bible Society 1976; New Testament: Copyright © American Bible Society 1966, 1971, 1976. Used by permission.

Quotations marked NASB are from the *New American Standard Bible*. Copyright © The Lockman Foundation, 1960, 1962, 1963, 1968, 1971, 1972, 1973, 1975, 1977. Used by permission.

Quotations marked NIV are from the HOLY BIBLE *New International Version,* copyright © 1978, New York Bible Society. Used by permission.

Quotations marked Phillips are reprinted with permission of Macmillian Publishing Co., Inc. from J. B. Phillips: *The New Testament in Modern English,* Revised Edition. © J. B. Phillips 1958, 1960, 1972.

Quotations marked RSV are from the Revised Standard Version of the Bible, copyrighted 1946, 1952, © 1971, 1973.

Quotations marked Williams are from *The New Testament, a Translation in the Language of the People,* by Charles B. Williams. Copyright 1937 and 1966. Moody Press, Moody Bible Institute of Chicago. Used by permission.

CONTENTS

About the Authors

Dr. Findley B. Edge of Winter Park, Florida, is a former professor of religious education at the Southern Baptist Theological Seminary, Louisville, Kentucky. During his years at Southern he influenced many pastors, ministers of education, ministers of youth, missionaries, and others in various fields of ministry. Since his retirement he has been much in demand as a writer and speaker in the area of ministry by the *laos* (the people of God).

Dr. Edge has written four outstanding books widely used by teachers and trainers in the church life—*Teaching for Results, Helping the Teacher, A Quest for Vitality in Religion,* and *The Greening of the Church.*

Mic Morrow is the writer of the teaching guide. He is an editor of adult curriculum materials for the Church Training Department, Sunday School Board of the Southern Baptist Convention, Nashville, Tennessee. Mic is the creator of two Broadman educational games for adults, *Opinion* and *Suppose.*

Introduction

The doctrine of the priesthood of all believers is a fundamental belief among Baptists. The doctrine of the laity derives from the priesthood of all believers or is another way of stating it. In recent years this doctrine has been a topic of major importance among many religious groups. The doctrine of the laity is so important, that if adequately understood and properly expressed in the life of God's people, it could bring about a spiritual awakening that would revolutionize the life and ministry of the church.

Laity is a word derived from *laos*, a Greek word meaning people. It is used most of the time in the phrase "the people of God" or "God's people." Laity includes all people who believe in and are committed to Jesus as Savior and Lord. The *laos*, then, includes church leaders such as pastor.

There is another Greek word, *laikos*, which means a layperson who is untrained, inferior, amateurish. This word is never used in the Old Testament. *Laos* is the New Testament word describing the people of God. From this we get a picture that God's people are to be equipped and trained people for ministry.

Among all mainline denominations, probably Southern Baptists emphasize and practice the doctrine of the laity as much as any and more than most. Often other religious groups are amazed that Southern Baptists are able to enlist such a large number of members to work in leadership capacities in church organizations. I want to affirm these people, many of whom give unselfishly of themselves in dedication and devotion in the work of Christ. We rejoice in their dedication and thank God for their service.

One may ask, If we are doing so well that others sometimes envy our success in this area, what is the problem? What is our weakness?

I will deal with what I feel are our major weaknesses and suggest ways we can strengthen these areas. However, I will mention here two problems we face in common with other religious groups. We as Southern Baptists have done well in enlisting the laity to serve in the organizational life of our churches. We have, however, tended to be weak in giving laypeople help in knowing how to be ministers in the marketplace and other areas of our society.

The second problem we face in common with the other denominations is, We are in danger of losing the battle for the ministry of the laity by default. For more than twenty-five years this doctrine has been proclaimed from pulpits, in books, and in journals. But the fact that a biblical truth is discussed does not at all guarantee that it is incorporated into the life and work of the churches. We are in danger of talking the ministry of the laity to death.

I consider myself to be a positive person rather than a negative one. Therefore it would not be difficult for me to point out numerous good and positive things about our churches. However, in this book I have chosen to point out where we have missed the mark with reference to this doctrine. I have sought to focus on the unfinished tasks. Therefore there are places where I may seem to be critical. If I am critical, it is with a view to making something positive come from it. My purpose is to provide a stimulus for insights to emerge, for conviction to take place, for change to occur, and for us to fulfill more fully God's call in our lives.

Chapter 1 asks the question, What does it really mean to be God's people? As a part of this overall question: If God's people are a unique people, as we claim to be, what is the essence of that uniqueness? Related to that is the question, What is the difference between being a religious people and being God's people? or Is there any difference? This chapter seeks to point out how imperative it is for us to understand what it means to be God's people.

Chapter 2 raises another pivotal question: If God's people are His basic ministers, how are they to be motivated to accept and fulfill this ministry? What is an adequate foundation for this motivation?

Chapter 3 asks, Who is the basic minister in your church? To whom does God give the responsibility for fulfilling His mission of reconciliation? Who were the ones who expressed the ministry of fulfilling God's mission? Can one fulfill one's ministry fully by giving money to the church? How is the doctrine of incarnation related to ministry?

Chapter 4 asks the question: If Christians are called by God to

10

fulfill His redemptive mission, what is the nature of the redemptive mission we are to be about? Does God's mission include human brokenness of people? Does God's mission also include the social ills which cause human brokenness?

In chapter 5 we raise the question, If the layperson is the basic minister of God's mission, what is the role of the pastor? What are some biblical teachings concerning the pastor's equipping role in the life of the church? Is it possible for one person to fulfill in any adequate sense all of the responsibilities we have placed upon the pastor? How did it come about that we gave the task of doing the ministry to the pastor? Does the emphasis on the ministry of the laity minimize the role of the pastor?

Chapter 6 deals with this question: If the layperson is God's basic minister to carry out His mission in the world, how can the layperson do this and still make a living and have any time for family? How is ministry expressed, anyway?

Chapter 7 deals with the relationship of spiritual gifts and ministry. If every Christian has a gift, and if one's gift(s) is related to one's ministry, why has not the church emphasized this more? How may one go about discovering his or her gift(s)? In light of one's gift(s), how may one go about discerning one's ministry?

The last chapter is unique. The last chapter asks, What can and should we do as the result of this study? I have made suggestions for groups to consider and discuss. In this study the individual should determine what personal response he or she would like to make. This personal response is basic. But in addition each church as a community should make a response.

In most churches, if the doctrine of the laity is taken seriously, there will need to be changes in attitudes and approaches. For most of us, significant changes are not easily made. Yet the very purpose for studying *The Doctrine of the Laity* is to recognize some areas in which significant changes need to be made.

In writing this book I have taken excerpts from a number of articles, chapters, and books I have written. I am grateful for permission to use these materials.

CHAPTER 1

THE PEOPLE

OF GOD

THE PEOPLE OF GOD

It was in B.Y.P.U. (Baptist Young People's Union), as Church Training was called then, that I had my first experience in trying to understand the nature and meaning of the Christian life in any systematic way. The Better Speakers Tournament was presented to us as an opportunity for growth and development. There would be elimination events in our church, the association, and the state. The winner would go to Ridgecrest. A list of topics was given from which we might select one. The topic, "What It Means to Be a Christian," immediately caught my attention. We were to prepare a five-minute talk. I wrote down everything I knew about the Christian life. Then I borrowed books from my pastor and took notes. At this point the thing I remember most vividly was how difficult it was to get enough material to fill out five minutes. This would make a nice story if I could say I won a trip to Ridgecrest, but that was not the case. The fact is, of the two who entered the tournament in our church, I came in second. However, the purpose of the tournament was accomplished. Although I was not aware of it at the time, I had started on a search that was to be the basic thrust of my life. I believed deeply in Jesus as Savior and Lord of my life. I belonged to God. I made the claim to be a part of His people. But what did all of this mean in the practical way I lived my life? What does it really mean to be a Christian?

A Struggle for Answers

The pivotal struggle of my search for answers to this question came about the time we call the midpoint of life. A number of things converged in my intellectual life and in the world about me that caused this question to become the central focus of my life.

My problem was not associated with any doubt as to the existence of God nor was it related to any doubt concerning my salvation. Rather the problem centered around those of us who claimed to be

Christian. I had always believed that belonging to God is the most important relationship that a person can experience in this life. I believed that salvation is a life transforming experience, that a person who is "in Christ," is, in fact, "a new creation." I felt that these words were not just a cliché but a reality. I felt that God's people are a *unique* people.

However, during this period of struggle and searching, the question was formed in my mind, If God's people are a unique people, what is the essence of that uniqueness? So disturbing was this question that it would not permit any glib answers. It was one of those profound experiences that a person sometimes has with oneself. The question persisted and demanded an answer.

PERSONAL LEARNING ACTIVITY 1
How would you answer the question: If God's people are, in fact, a unique people what is the essence of that uniqueness? Write your answer here.

As Christians, we make the claim that we are different from all other people in the world. If that is true, what is it that we are; what is it that we have; what is it that we do that makes us different from all other people in the world? Immediately the answer came to mind: We believe in Jesus, and they do not. Certainly this is correct. But the question persisted. If belief in Christ is so fundamental and so pivotal, how does this belief express itself in practical terms? If believing in Christ makes us different from other people, then how is this belief expressed in daily life? Two answers flashed into my mind. First, a Christian should be good. That is, he or she should live a good, clean, moral life. The goodness of our life is a testimony to our commitment to Jesus as Lord. Second, we should be faithful to the church. As I reflected back over my life, it seemed to me that these two emphases were the major expressions of my Christian life. All of my life I had tried to live as good and moral a Christian life as was possible. And all of my life I had seriously tried to be faithful to my church.

There is certainly nothing wrong with either of these emphases as desirable expressions of one's Christian faith. Certainly it is desirable for a Christian to live as good, clean, and moral a life as is possible. We are enjoined by God to be a "holy people" and moral character is related to holiness. Likewise, it is certainly desirable for one to be faithful to the church. The Scripture says that Christ "loved the church, and gave himself for it" (Eph. 5:25).

But as I indicated, this was an agonizing and persistent question for me and answers that before seemed to be so obvious no longer seemed so obvious. As I reflected upon the answers I had given, I became aware that there were many people in the world who made no pretense of believing in God or Jesus who were just as moral as I was. Many people in our communities outwardly profess no faith in Christ and are highly moral people. They are as honest in their business relations as I am. They are as faithful in their marriage relations as I am. They are as generous in helping others as I am. I am aware that these people are not perfect, but neither am I. They get angry and so do I. There are people who have never made a public profession of faith in Christ who are just as moral as Christians. So I was forced to conclude that while a Christian certainly ought to strive to live as good and as moral a life as possible, this is not what makes the Christian unique.

But when I came to my second answer I thought I was on more solid ground. Christians attend church and are faithful to the church and non-Christians are not. The church was founded by our Lord and is central in God's divine purpose. The church is spoken of as "the body of Christ" of which Christ is the head. We are admonished to support the church, financially and otherwise. And we are told not to forsake "the assembling of ourselves together" (Heb. 10:25). So for one to be faithful in the support of the church is a matter of importance. Yet as I looked out on the world with its brokenness and need, I was certain that God was interested in something deeper than how I relate to the church as an institution. And so my second answer also was not adequate.

There I was somewhere near the midpoint of my life. I was a Christian. I was a teacher in one of our seminaries. And yet I did not know the answer to the question which I felt every Christian ought to know, namely, if God's people are a unique people, what is the essence of that uniqueness?

God Works Through Individuals

God began wooing humankind back to Himself by calling a man— Abraham. We have an account of this call in Genesis 12:1-3:

Now the Lord had said unto Abram, Get thee out of thy country, and from thy kindred, and from thy father's house, unto a land that I will shew thee: And I will make of thee a great nation, and I will bless thee, and make thy name great; and thou shalt be a blessing: And I will bless them that bless thee, and curse him that curseth thee: and in thee shall all families of the earth be blessed.

In these three verses God makes at least two pivotal revelations. First, in the last part of verse 3 God reveals His purpose, what He is about. He says, "All families of the earth [are to] be blessed." God's purpose is all people everywhere are to know Him as God and Father. God wants to remake, to redeem that which has been marred by sin. God is seeking to bring wholeness to His people, indeed to the whole created order.

How is God going to do this? This is His second revelation. In the latter part of verse 2 God says to Abraham, "Thou shalt be a blessing." We need to note here that God's basic call to Abraham was not a call to accept something or to receive something. The *basic* call of Abraham was a call to mission—God's mission of reconciliation. This covenant was repeated to Abraham's son Isaac and to Isaac's son Jacob.

Jacob had twelve sons one of whom was Joseph. Joseph was sold by his brothers into slavery and was taken to Egypt. After a number of episodes Joseph was given a position of power. He brought his father, Jacob, and all the tribe to Egypt. They settled in the land of Goshen.

Four centuries passed and the tribe of Jacob multiplied to the point they became a threat to the internal security of the Egyptians. A ruler came to the throne who "knew not Joseph" (Ex. 1:8). The children of Israel were treated harshly and placed in bondage. The cry of the people was heard by God, and Moses was sent to lead the people out of bondage.

17

God Calls a People

Up to this point God had been working primarily through individuals—Abraham, Isaac, Jacob, Moses. Now God called a people. The people had been traveling for three months since their deliverance from Pharaoh (Ex. 19:1). Then they came to the base of Mt. Sinai. Moses went up into the mountain to meet God. God said to him, "Thus shalt thou say to the house of Jacob, and tell the children of Israel; ye have seen what I did unto the Egyptians, and how I bare you on eagles' wings, and brought you unto myself" (Ex. 19:3-4). To paraphrase, God said to Moses: "I want you to go back to the people and say to them, 'You have seen a demonstration of my might and power. You saw how I snatched you from the jaws of death and delivered you. You also have seen my watchcare over you. I have cared for you as though you were an eaglet on the wings of a mighty eagle.'"

God continued telling Moses what he, in turn, was to tell the people. "Now therefore, if [note the condition] ye will obey my voice indeed, and keep my covenant, then ye shall be a peculiar treasure unto me above all people: for all the earth is mine: And ye shall be unto me a kingdom of priests, and a holy nation. These are the words which thou shalt speak unto the children of Israel. And Moses came and called for the elders of the people, and laid before their faces all these words which the Lord commanded him. And all the people answered together, and said, All that the Lord hath spoken we will do" (Ex. 19:5-8). And so God and Israel entered into a covenant relationship.

Again there is a pivotal point we must note. Certainly gift and blessing were involved in this relationship. If they accepted God's call, they would be His people; and He would be their God. But, He was not offering a gift without condition. God said, "If you will . . ." What was the condition? Again, like with Abraham, God's basic call was a call to mission, a call to a task. God said, "You shall be to me a kingdom of priests. . . ." What is the function of a priest? One function is to be a mediator between God and the people. He is to stand between God on the one hand and a sinful people on the other and seek to bring the people and God together.

God was calling Israel to be a people of priests in terms of His redemptive purpose that all the people of the earth might be blessed. Would they do it? The response of the people was, "All that the Lord hath spoken we will do."

For a people (or a person) to say, "All that the Lord hath spoken, we will do," is one thing. It is quite another thing to carry it out.

Evidently Israel did not adequately understand the nature of God's call. In terms of the call of God in their lives it seems they heard only the blessing aspect. Seemingly they felt that in this relationship to which they had been called, God was to do all of the giving; and all they had to do was to receive. Whatever the reason or reasons, Israel failed to carry out the purpose for which they had been called. They took God for their own possession. They accepted Him. They believed Him. They even worshiped Him. But they failed to become a kingdom of priests to be a blessing to all the families of the earth.

However, the most stinging and ominous confrontation God had with Israel is recorded by Isaiah in his first chapter. The setting was a court scene. Israel was on trial, and God was the prosecuting attorney. He called for all of heaven and earth to be the jury. In Isaiah 1:2 God said: "Hear, O heavens, and give ear, O earth: for the Lord hath spoken." God then began His accusation, "I have nourished and brought up children, and they have rebelled against me. The ox knoweth his owner, and the ass his master's crib: but Israel doth not know, my people doth not consider" (Isa. 1:2b-3).

God then began to list the charges against His people. They were a people laden with iniquity. God stated that hope is to be found only in "a very small remnant" (v. 9).

In verse 11 and following, God became more specific in His charges. If the first chapter of Isaiah was to be made into a dramatic presentation, I think at verse 11 God's voice would become filled with satire. I think He would say, "You are such a religious people. As an expression of your religiosity you have this variety of sacrifices you make to me. The fact is, I am fed up with these offerings of rams and bullocks, and lambs and goats. This is not why I called you. You have completely misunderstood the purpose of my call and what you are to do to fulfill it." Skipping to verse 13, I think God would continue: "When you gather to worship, you burn incense as an expression of your devotion to me. As the sweet smelling odor rises, this is to be symbolic of your love and your worship. You need to know that, instead of being worshipful, this is offensive to me. It is offensive because you have misunderstood how your devotion is to be expressed. All your religious observances are a burden to me. Even when you lift up your hands in prayer, I will not listen. All of these things you do to worship me, to express your love for and devotion to me. The problem is, they have the reverse effect upon me—I hate them! I hate them not because they are not valid expressions of worship. I hate them not because I do not desire to be worshiped in this way. I hate them because this is not what I called you to be! This is not what I called you to do! You have become a religious people rather than an obedient people! Certainly I desire the love, devotion, and worship of my people; but when my people use worship as a means of evading the basic purpose for which I called you, then worship itself becomes a sin. I called you to be my people with all the gifts and blessings this involves. But behind the gifts there was a more fundamental call. I called you to a mission—my redemptive mission. I called you to join with me to be a kingdom of priests, to bring healing to the brokenness of the world, that all the families of the earth might find the blessing that only I can give. You said you would do it, but you failed—tragically failed. Instead you became a religious people."

In the last part of verse 15 God brought His final accusation against Israel, "Your hands are full of blood." Does this mean that the people had been guilty of murder? That and more. Does it mean that the people had been grossly immoral people? Not necessarily. We have to go to Ezekiel to get the full significance of this accusation. In Ezekiel 3:16-18 we read:

And it came to pass at the end of seven days, that the word of the Lord came unto me, saying, Son of man, I have made thee a watchman unto the house of Israel: therefore hear the word at my mouth, and give them warning from me. When I say unto the wicked, thou shalt surely die; and thou givest him not warning, nor speakest to warn the wicked from his wicked way, to save his life; the same wicked man shall die in his iniquity; but his blood will I require at thine hand.

In effect God said, I had called you to bless you. I had called you to give myself to you as you were to give yourself to me. But the purpose of my call and the basis of this relationship was you were to be a kingdom of priests. I had called you to give yourselves to be an instrument I could use to bring healing to the people of the world who had been broken by sin. You said you would do it. But you failed—tragically failed. You have been a very religious people and an evil people as well.

What, then, is Israel to do? God told them in verses 16 and 17 of Isaiah 1: "Wash you, make you clean; put away the evil of your doings from before mine eyes; cease to do evil; Learn to do well; seek judgment, relieve the oppressed, judge the fatherless, plead for the widow." God told Israel that they are to wash their hands and try to get them clean from the blood of those whom they had failed to warn. Also they were to cease to do evil. We tend to think of evil in terms of some form of immorality. However, the evil to which God refers here is the failure of Israel to fulfill the purpose for which God had called them. The evil which God wanted them to cease was their failure to be the instrument of His redemptive purpose He wanted them to be. When He said, "Learn to do well," He meant He wanted them to start fulfilling the purpose He stated in His call to Abraham and stated in His call to them as a people, to be "a kingdom of priests" (Ex. 19:6) that "all the families of the earth [might] be blessed" (Gen. 12:3).

How was this to be done? He told them clearly. They were to seek justice and help those who are needy and oppressed. They were to care for the orphans and the widows. God said for them to begin caring for and ministering to the broken people of the world. That is what He is about and that is what He called them to be about.

PERSONAL LEARNING ACTIVITY 2
In what way or ways is the situation in our churches similar to that of Israel? Please list.

In what way or ways is the situation in our churches different from that of Israel? Please list.

Unfortunately, in spite of the warning of God and the teachings of the prophets, Israel continued in her misunderstanding of the kind of people God meant for them to be when He called them to be His people.

Jesus Confronts the Scribes and Pharisees

In His ministry Jesus sought to explain the kind of God the Heavenly Father is. There were some who believed even among the chief priests, scribes, and Pharisees. The common people heard Him gladly and many believed—until He gave some of His hard teachings. But it was with the religious leaders that Jesus had His most serious conflicts. In Matthew 21 we see this conflict as it moves toward its inevitable climax. Jesus made His triumphal entry into Jerusalem: "And a very great multitude spread their garments in the way; others cut down branches from the trees, and strawed them in the way" (v. 8). The people shouted their hosannas; and when the chief priests and scribes saw the response of the people, "they were sore displeased" (v. 15). The next day the chief priests and elders challenged His authority for the things He was doing.

The authority of Jesus to do His work came from God. The Pharisees rejected the idea that Jesus had this authority. It was inconceivable to them that the Messiah would be anything like this man from Galilee. They rejected Him because His message was one of love and not of retribution. Within Jesus' message of love was a call to mission.

It must be understood that this conflict over the nature of God had been building over a period of approximately three years. In the parable of the two sons (vv. 28-32) Jesus again confronted them with their tragic misunderstanding of what God is about and what He calls His people to be. This is evidenced by the reaction of the Pharisees, who, among the religious leaders, had the strongest influence over the people. Now, I have no desire to paint an unfair picture of the Pharisees. They were the choicest spirits of Judaism of Jesus' day. Actually, they were a highly moral people, deeply dedicated to religion as they understood it. They came into existence two hundred years earlier as a reform movement because the average Israelite was not keeping the commandments of God with care and devotion. The Pharisees were a group who separated themselves from the common people and dedicated themselves to the strict observance of God's law. Indeed this is precisely the point of their misunderstanding of God's call. They thought God had called them to be a *separated people* rather than a *people on mission*. The danger our churches face today is exactly this same misunderstanding.

The fact is, Judaism had an evangelistic thrust. Throughout the Graeco-Roman world they sought proselytes to the Jewish faith (Matt. 23:15a). However, theirs was a type of exclusive evangelism—an evangelism on their own terms. They would accept those who were willing to become separated from the world and who would give themselves with devoted concern to institutional observance and ceremonial purity. But they did not understand that they were called by God to be instruments of His caring love—thrust into the world, not separated from the world—to love people where they were and as they were. The Pharisees were willing to welcome sinners *after* they repented. The revolutionary demonstration of Jesus was that He loved sinners *before* they repented. This is the way God loves, and this is the way God is calling His people to love. To love like this is their mission because it is God's mission. Their problem was clearly indicated in the two parables Jesus told. In the first parable (Matt. 21:28-32) Jesus said a certain father had two sons. He said to the first, Go work in my vineyard. This son refused. He said, I will not. But later he repented and went. Then he said the same thing to the second son, Go work in my vineyard. This son said, I will do it. But he did not! In this parable, the vineyard, of course, is the world. The second son is Israel. When God called Israel to be His people (Ex. 19:3-8), He called them to work in His vineyard (the world) to fulfill His mission in the world, "that . . . all the families of the earth be blessed" (Gen. 12:3). They said they would do it but they did not! They were a religious people but they did not fulfill His call.

The second parable begins in verse 33. To paraphrase again, the parable tells about a certain man who built a vineyard and let it out to workers. He went into a far country. When the time of harvest came, he sent some of his servants to receive the fruits of it. But the workers in the vineyard stoned and killed these servants. The owner of the vineyard sent still more servants, and they were stoned and killed also. Finally the owner of the vineyard said, "I know what I will do. I will send my son. Surely these people will reverence my son." But the workers in the vineyard heard that the son was coming, and they said, "Let's kill him and take the whole thing for ourselves." The meaning of this parable is rather self-evident. The owner of the vineyard is God. The vineyard, again, is the world. The workers are the people whom God called to be His people, Israel. The son was Jesus. When Jesus finished telling the parable, He turned to the people who were standing around and instead of asking them the meaning of the parable He asked them, "What do you think the owner of the vineyard will do to these workers in the vineyard?" They replied, "Why, he will destroy those evil men."

Then follows what I consider to be one of the most pivotal, important, and significant verses in all of the Bible. Jesus is speaking to the scribes and Pharisees who are the official representatives of Judaism. God and Israel are once again facing each other in direct confrontation. Jesus said, "Therefore say I unto you, the kingdom of God shall be taken from you, and given to a nation bringing forth the fruits thereof" (v. 43). In effect Jesus said to Israel, for more than a thousand years you have had your chance. God called you for a purpose. God said, go work in my vineyard. Be a kingdom of priests. You said you would do it, but you failed. Therefore the kingdom is taken from you and given to a people who *will* bring forth fruit—that is, who will fulfill the purpose of their calling.

The New Israel

God calls the new Israel to be His people, and you and I make the audacious claim that we are a part of this new Israel of God. But the thing we must understand with clarity is, the new Israel is called for precisely the same purpose as was the original Israel. Basic in our call is a call to a task. *We are called to a mission.*

Early in this chapter we raised the question, "If God's people are a unique people, what is the essence of that uniqueness?" It has been stated several times through the chapter. Let us state it once more in the conclusion. Certainly God's people believe in God, but that is not the essence of their uniqueness. Certainly they are a people who are good in terms of their personal morality. But that is not the essence of their uniqueness. Certainly they are a religious people, but that is not the essence of their uniqueness. The uniqueness of God's people is they are a people who have been called to a mission—God's mission! This is clearly understood. They have joyfully accepted this mission and have given their lives to its fulfillment. The people of God believe that what God is seeking to do in the lives of people and in the world is what is desperately needed. They believe this so deeply and with such commitment that their lives are joyfully given to God as instruments in seeking to cause the will of God to be "done on earth as it is in heaven." This is the nature of their uniqueness. In living life this way, in losing their lives for the gospel's sake, they find Jesus is absolutely correct—in their own lives they find healing, wholeness, meaning, blessings, life in increasing abundance!

24

PERSONAL LEARNING ACTIVITY 3
What is your reaction to the author's answer to the question, "If God's people are a unique people, what is the essence of that uniqueness?" Whether you agree or disagree, please indicate why.

CHAPTER 2

MOTIVATION

LAITY

FOR MINISTRY

CHAPTER 2

LAITY

MOTIVATION FOR MINISTRY

The emphasis in this study has been on the fact that the laity are the basic ministers of God's mission of reconciliation in the world. Pastors, however, may protest, saying this is not a new emphasis. In their preaching, teaching, and ministry, this is what they have been trying to get the laity to do all along. Certainly I am aware that they have preached dedication, commitment, and involvement. Thank God many have heard and responded. We recognize these and affirm the ministry they have rendered. Unfortunately, the total number who have responded has been quite limited.

Where can we find a motivation that is able to transform members into ministers? I would like to suggest for your consideration that our basic problem regarding a lack of motivation stems from a limited understanding of the salvation relationship. More specifically it comes from an approach to the conversion experience that too often has tended to be shallow. The problem which the doctrine of the laity points up is this—we have not understood adequately that God's call to become a part of His people is also a call to ministry. We have emphasized God's gift and God's grace, both of which are correct, but we have not given an adequate emphasis to God's call to ministry for every Christian.

The pastor's message in the pulpit has been both correct and forceful. The Christian and the potential convert are told that they must be willing to lay their lives on the altar for Christ; they must be willing to deny self; they must take up their cross and follow Christ; they must be willing to die daily. If taken seriously, this is a demanding and challenging life to which one is called. But where is the acceptance of a call to ministry?

God's Call in the Conversion Experience

Our problem of motivation centers in a limited understanding of the conversion experience. Too many have accepted the gift of salvation without making a commitment to be involved. And so pastors and other church leaders are trying to motivate people to be involved who see absolutely no relationship between this involvement and their conversion experience.

This is the point where our reformation is to come. This is where and how we can help complete the reformation started by Martin Luther in 1513. Among other things, Luther opened the Bible to the laity. But his efforts to open the ministry to the laity were not fulfilled. Now, in our generation, if we are sufficiently daring and have the commitment, we can open the ministry to the laity. But, if we are going to have a commitment and a relationship with Christ that is adequate to motivate people to give themselves to that ministry, it is necessary that we have a deeper view of the salvation relationship and the conversion experience.

The problem in our churches is not that we do not have enough members. Our problem is we do not have enough ministers. We will not have enough ministers unless our members have a deeper motivation. They will not have a deeper motivation until there is a deeper understanding of God's call in the salvation relationship.

What is the biblical view of conversion? What do we need to understand? What is the nature of the commitment we need to make? Let me share with you my understanding of the biblical perspective in this tremendously important area. We cannot be exhaustive in this study, but perhaps we can be suggestive.

The Meaning of Faith

Southern Baptists and others who hold an evangelical understanding of the gospel recognize that faith is a fundamental part of being saved. Indeed, it is the essential ingredient in one's salvation relationship. Scripture after Scripture points to the centrality and necessity of faith in the salvation relationship with God through Christ. One's eternal destiny is determined by the reality and authenticity of this relationship; therefore, there probably is nothing in one's total religious experience that is of a more decisive importance. Therefore, it is understandable why faith has been a central emphasis in the preaching and teaching that has been done in our churches.

However, the emphasis in our churches has been primarily on exhortation rather than on explanation. The emphasis has been on exercising faith rather than on understanding faith. In the preaching and teaching in our churches, we have exhorted people to "have faith," "to trust," "to believe," as though everyone understood quite clearly what these phrases meant. Although our emphasis on the necessity of having faith has been strong and quite sincere, our understanding of what the New Testament means by "having faith" has tended to be much too superficial and therefore tragically limited.

In seeking to understand what the New Testament means by faith as related to the salvation relationship, certain passages suggest that the salvation relationship is a relatively simple and easy relationship to enter. For example, "Except ye be converted; and become as little children, ye shall not enter into the kingdom of heaven" (Matt. 18:3). "God so loved the world, that he gave his only begotten Son, that whosoever believeth in him should not perish, but have everlasting life" (John 3:16). On the other hand, there are passages that seem to indicate that the salvation relationship is difficult and terribly demanding and that one should enter this relationship only after the most careful assessment of the cost involved in terms of one's life. For example, "Enter ye in at the strait gate: . . . because strait is the gate, and narrow is the way, which leadeth unto life, and few there be that find it" (Matt. 7:13-14). "What shall I do that I may inherit eternal life? . . . Jesus said unto him, . . . sell whatsoever thou hast . . . and follow me" (Mark 10:17-21).

Both of these emphases are true and necessary aspects in a correct understanding of the nature of the salvation relationship and must be held in proper balance. One cannot say in one statement everything that needs to be said about a complex relationship. Only from a consideration of all that is written about the nature of and what is involved in the salvation relationship can we come to understand what the New Testament means by having faith.

Two passages seem to illustrate this dual emphasis of gift and response in the salvation relationship. One is Ephesians 2:8-9: "By grace are ye saved through faith; and that not of yourselves: it is the gift of God: not of works, lest any man should boast." The other is James 2:14,20: "What doth it profit, my brethren, though a man say he has faith, and have not works? can faith save him? But wilt thou know, O vain man, that faith without works is dead?" The Ephesians passage emphasizes salvation as gift. This salvation relationship is God's work based on man's response of faith. The James passage says there is a faith that is not authentic and therefore not salvific, having the intent or power to save or redeem. Even Jesus indicated there was a faith that was not authentic. "Not every one that saith unto me, Lord, Lord, shall enter into the kingdom of heaven" (Matt. 7:21).

30

As Southern Baptists with all our emphasis on evangelism, the necessity of salvation in the life of every person, and the centrality of faith in the salvation relationship, we have not dealt adequately with the questions, What is the essence of authentic faith? How does it differ from inauthentic faith? It is almost unbelievable that a religious group could hold an emphasis to be so central in its belief system as we hold faith and yet treat its meaning so lightly. The question is complex and difficult. It is to this question we now turn our attention. This question is directly related and fundamental to the problem of motivation with which this chapter deals. The difficulty in our churches is that we may be trying to motivate people to become involved in something to which they never have committed themselves. Therefore, what we need is not gimmicks or bribes to entice them; what we need is to lead them in a basic reexamination of their conversion experience, their basic commitment to Jesus Christ.

Salvation is gift. Paul said that salvation is "by grace"; it is on the basis of God's unmerited favor. The image of God in which we were created, which has been marred by sin, can only be restored by God. This alienation from God and this brokenness in our human existence which we have brought upon ourselves by sin can only be remedied by an act of God.

Not only does this salvation come to us by an act of God, it is God who takes the initiative for this salvation in our behalf. The Bible says, "While we were yet sinners, Christ died for us" (Rom. 5:8). Jesus said that the Father is like a shepherd who is so concerned for one sheep that is lost that he leaves all the rest and goes searching for it until he finds it. He is like a woman who searches diligently for a lost coin. He is like a father who yearns for a straying son.

Not only is this salvation by an act of God and from the initiative of God, it is gift. We do not merit this gracious gift of God; neither can we earn it by our works of righteousness. We human beings, with all of our potential, are reminded that there are simply some things we cannot do. Jesus pointed this out when He asked, "Which of you by taking thought can add one cubit to his stature?" (Matt. 6:27). We can till the soil and weed the crops, but the *source* of the growth process is not found within our work. If we sustain a major cut on some part of our body, we can do a number of things to try to keep infection away; but the *source* of the healing process is not ours to command. The brokenness in our lives caused by sin can be healed only by an act of God. It is gift!

The gift—is it conditional or unconditional? This gift, which we

31

neither merit nor can earn, is it conditional or is it unconditional? We seem to feel, either consciously or unconsciously, that if in any way a condition is attached, something significant has been taken away from the giftedness of salvation. Indeed, when we preach, inviting people into this salvation relationship, in our emphasis on the reality of "gift" we say, "It is *wholly* gift." What we mean when we say this is that this salvation is all the work of God. And, of course, this is true. But, too often what we imply *by what is left unsaid,* is that there is nothing we have to do in terms of response. Our emphasis is on accepting the gift.

So we need to ask, from a biblical perspective, Is there or is there not a condition attached to this gift of salvation? This, it seems to me, is a pivotal question in seeking an answer to the larger question, What is involved in an authentic faith?

Traditionally, Southern Baptists have rejected the view of infant baptism. We have insisted on "believers baptism." By this we have meant that an individual comes into an authentic relationship with God, through Christ, only on the basis of a free, conscious, self-chosen decision. By *free* we mean that the individual in making his or her decision for Christ must not be under any form of duress, or pressure, or manipulation. By *conscious* we mean the individual must be sufficiently mature to be conscious of what is involved in this decision and be conscious of what he or she is doing in accepting Jesus as Savior. We mean that the individual must be sufficiently mature to be aware that he or she is a sinner before God, be conscious of God as a loving Father, and be conscious of Jesus as Lord and Savior. By *self chosen* we mean that the decision must be personal. This decision cannot be made by proxy, not by mother, father, husband, wife, or anyone else. So intimate is this relationship in the salvation experience that it can be entered into only by the individual himself or herself.

However, when we as Southern Baptists say that for one to be saved it is necessary for one to make a free, self-conscious, personal choice, we also say that salvation is conditional. The condition is, one must make a choice. When we say one must "accept Christ," or when we say one must "make a response" to God's invitation, we state there is a condition that must be met before we can receive this salvation. To state the matter from God's perspective, there is a condition that must be met before God can or will give His gift of salvation.

Understanding the condition. The question, then, before us is,

What is the nature of the condition that the New Testament places on the salvation relationship?

According to the Bible, the central condition for the salvation relationship is for the individual to have faith/believe. Numerous passages attest to this fact. When the Philippian jailor cried out, "Sirs, what must I do to be saved?" the reply was, "Believe on the Lord Jesus Christ, and thou shalt be saved, and thy house" (Acts 16:30-31).

Believing/having faith is the central condition for the salvation relationship. It becomes a matter of prime importance to answer with clarity the question, What does the Bible mean by *having faith* and *believe*?

First, we have a linguistic problem; that is, a problem related to the meaning of words. In the New Testament, the Greek word for *faith* in its noun form is *pistis* and in its verb form is *pisteuo*. Both words come from the same root word. Unfortunately, in our English language, we do not have a verb form for the word *faith* (that is, I faith, you faith, he faiths). Therefore, in 1611 when those who translated the King James Version of the Bible came to the verb form of the Greek word for *faith,* they translated it *believe.* This would not have created a problem except that in the intervening centuries the word *believe* has had a rather significant change in meaning. This seemingly simple change in meaning has had, in my judgment, a profound effect on evangelical Christianity since that time and may be one of the major causes for weakness in our approach to evangelism today. In 1611 *to believe* meant to hold dear, to give one's allegiance to, to give oneself to. It was the committing of oneself to another as in a marriage relationship. The meaning of the word was highly personal and involved a depth relationship. Today, however, the word *believe* has come to mean primarily the cognitive acceptance of some proposition. It is true that we talk about being related to God personally and "giving ourselves to God," but in too many instances the primary meaning of *believe* is a belief in propositions about God. Belief in God means we believe in His existence. Belief in Jesus as Savior means an intellectual belief that Jesus can and will save us. One of the major weaknesses in our churches today is the tendency to make salvation a cognitive belief in a set of propositions.

This tendency has created a corollary problem for us, namely, the tendency to view salvation primarily as a status. These two problems have fed each other. Because we have tended to view salvation as a status rather than as a dynamic relationship, we sometimes have been guilty of devising our own plan for salvation. By the careful selection of the Scripture passages we use, we have tended to manipulate people into making professions of faith; and then we have placed on God the responsibility of honoring our plan, on the authority of the Word of God. If we can get people to "believe in Jesus," then on the basis of God's Word he or she is received into the kingdom of God and is secure for eternity.

It is true, there is a sense in which salvation is a status. We have been delivered out of bondage and declared by God to be "sons of God" and "joint-heirs with Christ." Our status has been forever changed by God. But we have this status because of a relationship; and this relationship is alive, dynamic, and growing. This relationship demands commitment and continuing response on our part. This gift of salvation is not given casually by God. It is not given simply on the basis of a cognitive belief in Jesus as Savior. The relationship between the individual and Christ is so intimate, so personal, so dynamic that it is, as Frank Stagg says, "beyond anything known within the natural family." Jesus said, "He that loveth father or mother more than me is not worthy of me: and he that loveth son or daughter more than me is not worthy of me" (Matt. 10:37). Again Jesus said, "If any man come to me, and hate not his father, and mother, and wife, and children, and brethren, and sisters, yea, and his own life also, he cannot be my disciple" (Luke 14:26). These verses speak of a relationship and commitment that are deeper and more intimate than the loyalty one has for one's family. The Luke verse speaks of a relationship and a commitment that are so deep and intimate that one is willing to risk one's life (literally) to obey and fulfill the purpose of God in the world. This seems to me to be a very deep and intimate relationship.

Along with the linguistic problem, there is a second major problem in understanding the condition of an authentic "in Christ" relationship. If one's commitment to Christ involves a commitment to fulfill that to which God calls us, our weakness has been a failure to make adequately clear to the potential convert that to which God is calling us when He calls us to be a part of His people. We have emphasized the necessity of being related to Christ personally, but what does it mean to be related to Christ personally? We cannot be related to Christ in a vacuum. We have to be related to Him in terms of something. This is what *be related to* means. Let me illustrate. Here is a person who, at the risk of his life, is leading an underground movement against the oppression of communism in one of the countries behind the Iron Curtain in Europe. His wife is "related to him personally" in a relationship of human love and marriage. She may not be "related" (committed) to him in terms of what he is about as the leader of a movement against communism. On the other hand, here is a young man who is also "related to the leader personally," but he is related to him in terms of what he (the leader) is about. Thus, our relationship to another, because it is a personal relationship, must be in terms of something. It seems to me at the present time in our evangelistic emphasis, our relationship to Christ has been primarily in terms of what we get. That is, we are related to Christ in terms of what He can do (or does) for us. As the song "My Jesus I Love Thee" by William R. Featherstone says:

I love him, I love him because he first loved me,
And purchased my salvation on Calvary's tree.

But someone may protest that we love God because He is God, that we love Him because of who He is. That someone says we love Him because He is worthy of love. It is my contention that it is because of who He is and what He is about that makes Him worthy of love. *Who God is* cannot be separated from what God is about.

This means that if we are going to be related to God in an authentic way, we must not only be related to Him in terms of what He gives, we must also be related to Him in terms of what He is about, namely, His mission in the world. Again, let me try to illustrate what it means to believe in Jesus.

In your imagination, picture Jesus and a young man sitting on a hillside, engaged in earnest conversation. The young man has heard Jesus teach on many occasions and, indeed, has had numerous personal conversations with Him. Finally Jesus says, "What you must decide is whether you really *believe* in Me or not." When Jesus asks this young man "to believe," I think He is saying: "Do you believe in the kind of God I am teaching about (revealing) as distinguished from the kind of God you have been taught about in the synagogues? Do you believe that the God who relates to people and who teaches people to relate to one another in the way I have taught and related to people is, in reality, the true God? Are you willing, as I am doing, to give your life to what God is trying to do in the world?" In this imaginary scene, when Jesus asks the young man "to believe," He is asking him to be related to, to be committed to the God who was doing these kinds of things and seeking these kinds of relationships among all people—the kinds of relationships Jesus was expressing in His own life.

Now we are coming close to finding what I think is the essence of authentic faith as distinguished from inauthentic faith. Authentic faith is the faith that emphasizes both the gift of salvation and the personal relationship with God in which one accepts and fulfills the call of God in terms of who God is and what God is about.

Our Response

Our response is to have faith that involves a personal relationship with Christ and a commitment to Him. It means we are to be willing even to risk our lives to fulfill what God is about in the world. Based on these truths, it is important to understand with some clarity who God is and what He is about in the world.

Our God is both Creator and Father, who loves His creation, marred and broken though it is. His eternal purpose is to redeem and bring healing to this brokenness. His purpose and plan for accomplishing this purpose were announced in His call of Abraham (Gen. 12:1-3). He later called Israel to be His unique people. Their uniqueness was to be found in their mission. They were to be a "kingdom of priests" (Ex. 19:1-8). Unfortunately, Israel misunderstood the nature of God's call; and instead of becoming a people on mission to fulfill God's mission, they became a religious people. They thought God had called them to bless them. They believed in God. They worshiped God. They sought to be faithful in carrying out their religious observances. They were warned by Isaiah and others, but they persisted in their failure. Jesus pronounced God's judgment upon them, and God called a "New Israel" (Matt. 21:43). The "New Israel," like the original Israel, was also called to fulfill God's mission of redemption in the world.

This divine mission of God was both spiritual and human. God's work in Christ did for us in terms of our spiritual relationship with Him what we were unable to do for ourselves. God, through Christ, also demonstrated that His mission included the love, care, and healing of people in their human situation.

All of the people, the *laos*, are called to be the ministers of this mission of reconciliation (2 Cor. 5:17-18; 1 Pet. 2:5,9). The doctrine of incarnation suggests that this ministry basically must be performed in person. It cannot be done by proxy.

Out from among the *laos*, God gifted and called some to be the teachers of His people, to equip them for their ministry (Eph. 4:11-12). Likewise, God gifted His people, each one of them, for the ministry each was to perform at a given time. It all fits together. The

36

design of God for the fulfillment of His mission in the world is so clear. We are grateful for those who devotedly give themselves to fulfilling this mission of reconciliation. Yet the large percent of church members do not understand that they have been called. Many refuse to become involved. We are aware of how we have "missed the mark" in understanding and fulfilling God's design for accomplishing His redemptive mission. We have secured many members, but we have not developed many ministers. And it was to be ministers God called us when He called us to be His people.

We have reviewed briefly these questions: What is God about in the world? When God calls us to be His people, what does He call us to be and do? Now we are ready to come back to the question that was left unanswered, What is the nature of authentic faith? According to the Bible authentic faith, as I understand it, is a commitment of one's life to God through Christ in a continuing and growing relationship. One hears and understands God's call to mission, both personal and social, and gives oneself to be an instrument to fulfill this mission in the world.

A second question is also related—Is accepting and fulfilling this mission *optional* for one who has an authentic "in Christ" relationship? My response to this is a clear and resounding no! Salvation is gift, wholly gift, but this gift is given only on the basis of the quality of response which God Himself sets. The One who called us to this mission and the fulfilling of it, who gifted us, who appointed some to equip us, and who empowers us and gives us His presence through the Holy Spirit *expects us to fulfill this mission when we say to Him, "I give You my life."'* Authentic faith is a faith that fulfills that to which God has called us.

Yet here we are in our churches, spending our time, energy, and thoughts seeking to find ways to entice our members into a program of Bible study and Christian development. We beg, we plead with them to take advantage of the opportunities for study and development we provide; and then we rejoice if a few of them respond. The late Paul "Bear" Bryant, was the widely known and popular coach of football at the University of Alabama. Can you imagine Coach "Bear" Bryant, after a game, saying to the team in a pleading voice: "Please come to practice next week. Last week we didn't have enough to come out so we could scrimmage. We just can't learn to play the game unless we practice, so please come out." Such a thought is ludicrous. If he said anything at all, it was something like: "Practice is at the regular time on Monday. Be there." Thus, we get from organized sports a basic principle for the church—*inherent in joining the team is a commitment to play the game. Inherent in the commitment to play the game is a commitment to practice.* This means that for the person who is "in Christ" growth and development for the ministry to which we are called is not optional. To have any less commitment in the salvation relationship and church membership, in my judgment, makes the Christian faith and the church a shallow mockery.

Two objections need a brief response. Some may object and say, "Do we not come to Christ as 'babes?'" It is not possible for us to understand all that we need to understand about mission and ministry when we first accept Jesus as Savior. It is true we do come to Christ as "babes." However, the inference that is implied in this question is, I think, erroneous. A human relationship can never illustrate adequately a spiritual relationship, but I hope this one may be suggestive. When I came to the point of making the decision to enter the marriage relationship with my "beloved," I came as a "babe" to this relationship. I certainly did not know all that was involved in a marriage relationship. But my commitment to my "beloved"—at the very beginning—was of such nature and of such depth that come what may, whatever was involved, I was committed to her for life. So it is with one's commitment to Christ as Lord and Savior. To fulfill that to which one is called is not optional for one who has an authentic "in Christ" relationship.

A second objection might be phrased, "Do you mean there are none who are saved at the present time?" This is certainly not what I am suggesting. Many in our churches are fulfilling God's mission of reconciliation. In addition, there are many others who are Christian even though they are not, in any conscious way, fulfilling God's mission in the world, because they have an authentic commitment to Christ. Their problem is, they have never been adequately taught. The laypeople in our churches today are what they are largely because of what those who were called to equip them have taught them.

The foundation for the motivation for ministry is found in the conversion experience. Those who do not have this motivation need to reexamine the clarity of their understanding of what they were committing themselves to and the depth of their commitment when they made their "profession of faith."

Notes

[1] Frank Stagg, *New Testament Theology* (Nashville: Broadman Press, 1962), p. 175.

PERSONAL LEARNING ACTIVITY 4

Do you believe there is a type of faith that is not authentic? If not, why not?

If you do believe there is a type of faith that is not authentic, how would you describe the difference between a faith that is authentic and a faith that is not authentic?

How did Jesus describe this difference? See Matthew 7:21-23.

Is accepting and fulfilling the mission for which God called us optional for one who has an authentic faith?

CHAPTER 3

THE MINISTRY

OF THE LAITY

CHAPTER 3

THE MINISTRY OF THE LAITY

In the previous chapter it was emphasized that God called a people to fulfill His redemptive mission. The people were responsible for being a blessing that all the families of the earth might be blessed. Therefore, we recognize today that all Christians have been called by God to serve and be a witness for Him. We recognize that all Christians are responsible for fulfilling God's redemptive purpose. Therefore, if we were to ask the question, Who has the basic responsibility for fulfilling God's mission in the world? the answer would seem to be rather obvious—the people!

But in my earlier years I would have been one of those who would have vigorously objected to this answer. Of course I recognized that everyone—all of God's people—have a responsibility to serve Him. That was not the basis for my objection. My objection would have been that out from among His people God has called a special group whom we call ministers to whom He gave the basic responsibility for fulfilling His mission in the world.

In my teen years I felt God's call in my life. I was convinced that what God was seeking to do in the world was what the world desperately needed. I wanted to give my life to Him to be an instrument He would use in accomplishing His will in the world. I wanted to serve Him full time. So I entered the ministry. I was aware that every Christian was called to serve God. But having entered the ministry, I was one of those specially called by God to do His ministry. While every Christian was responsible to a certain extent, I had now been called by God and given the basic responsibility for fulfilling God's mission in the world. I joyfully accepted this responsibility. I wanted to do God's work. I was willing to give Him my life to fulfill this responsibility.

As a senior in college, I became pastor of a small but deeply caring group of people. I accepted the responsibility of seeking to accomplish God's redemptive purpose in that place. Of course I sought to get many of the laypeople to help me in doing God's work. Thank God for that limited number who served God so willingly and effectively. Unfortunately most of the members simply attended on Sunday. I was the one who did most of the visiting. I was the one who did most of the evangelizing. I was the one who visited the prospects. I was the one who ministered to the sick and cared for the sorrowing. This was also the way things worked in the delightful church I served for nearly six years while a Southern Seminary student. Things worked the same way in the loving church I served for the two years I was an instructor at Southern Seminary. But that was all right with me. That was the way things were supposed to be. I was the one who had been called in a special way to fulfill God's purpose in the world. I had joyfully accepted this responsibility. Of course the people had some responsibility, but I was more responsible. It was I who had the basic responsibility for doing God's work in the world.

This would have been my answer up until the time I was approximately forty years old. During this same period of search in my life, I not only made a discovery about the uniqueness of God's people (a people on mission), I made a discovery about who are the basic ministers of that mission.

This leads us to a brief study of the doctrine of the priesthood of all believers. This doctrine has been one of our basic Baptist beliefs. Unfortunately our understanding of this great doctrine has tended to be too limited. Generally in our interpretation we have said that the priesthood of all believers means that as priests every Christian has the right of direct access to God.

During the Reformation, Martin Luther and other reformers emphasized the doctrine of the priesthood of all believers in opposition to the view of the clergy held by the Roman Catholic Church at that time. The Roman Church held that the laypersons must approach God through the mediation of a priest. For example, if a Roman Catholic wished to receive forgiveness for his or her sins, the person came to a priest, confessed the sins, and received absolution. However, the reformers reaffirmed what is clearly taught in Holy Scripture, namely, that every Christian is a priest. Therefore, if every Christian is a priest, then he/she does not need another priest to serve as a mediator between the person and God.

The Meaning of the Priesthood of All Believers

The above interpretation of this significant doctrine is certainly correct. The problem is, this interpretation does not give the full meaning of this doctrine. Martin Luther and other reformers did call attention to an additional teaching. But since the major problem they were confronting in this area was the question of a priestly mediator, their emphasis was on the right of all Christians (priests) to have direct access to God. In the centuries that have followed, though there have been a few attempts to broaden the meaning, the major emphasis has been on the right of direct access to God. This emphasis has been strong among Baptists and a few other denominations.

This concept of direct access to God is only a part of the doctrine of the priesthood of believers. The doctrine also means that in this direct access God is at work approaching the believer. As each Christian seeks his/her place in specific minstry, God makes clear His call to that specific ministry.

Another aspect of this doctrine has to do with the believer's responsibility to seek out his/her spiritual gift. This gift is to be used in ministry.

Along with this seeking out spiritual gifts, another aspect of the priesthood of believers has to be identified. The church has the responsibility of providing an adequate program for gift discovery to take place.

Affirmation of a believer's call on the part of the church is another aspect of this doctrine. The church as a body of baptized believers is responsible for affirming or not affirming an individual believer's call. The believer must then deal with this affirmation or non-affirmation in the light of his/her own understanding.

The doctrine of the priesthood of all believers also means that since every Christian is a priest, every Christian is therefore also a minister! Along the journey of my search when I made this discovery, it simply transformed my thinking and the emphasis of my ministry. First, I became aware of how mistaken I had been when I was pastor of those three small churches as to what the laypeople had been called by God to do and what I had been called to do. Second, I became convinced that if Southern Baptists (and other Christians) could come to understand this doctrine in the fullness of its meaning and if we were to express it in our lives, this doctrine would revolutionize the life and ministry of our churches.

The call to salvation and the call to ministry are two practical and very important points to be derived from this meaning of the priesthood of all believers. The first is, the call to salvation and the call to ministry are one and the same call. Let me hasten to add, so that I will not be misunderstood, there is another call from God for those who are called to the responsibility of specific church leadership.

The second practical point that is derived from the priesthood of all believers is equally, if not more, important. This doctrine means that the primary responsibility for God's ministry in the world rests upon the shoulders of the layperson and not upon the shoulders of the clergy!

It is my belief that the large majority of Southern Baptists do not agree with this point. They recognize that they have some responsibility for serving God but not the primary responsibility. They feel the primary responsibility belongs to the pastor and other staff. I think I can prove my point by using a hypothetical illustration. Although this illustration is hypothetical, it has happened so many times nearly everyone will think of a similar situation. In a given church, over a long period of time, the Sunday School attendance declines until finally only a very small number attend. The attendance at the worship services also declines and declines until only a faithful few are present on Sunday. Church Training, Brotherhood, and Woman's Missionary Union are all struggling with only a handful in attendance at the various meetings. It has been months that have lengthened into a year or more since there was a baptism. In fact, it has been longer than anyone can remember since anyone has even joined the church by letter. No one ever visits the church. At times the pastor and his wife are the only ones present at the midweek prayer service. The budget has declined year by year, and there are times when the pastor's salary cannot be paid. If this spirit of decline continues over an extended period of time, the deacons eventually will hold a secret meeting. By secret meeting, I mean the pastor will not be present. And the subject for this meeting is, "How can we get rid of the preacher?"

If I as an outsider were to be sitting in this secret meeting and if I were to ask, "Why do you want to get rid of the preacher?" the answer would be swift in coming: "He's simply not getting the work done! The church is dying!" They would begin to catalog his weaknesses and failures. Finally, they would conclude by saying something like: "We need a preacher who can attract the people. We need someone who can reach the people. We need a preacher who is evangelistic and who will visit the people!"

Certainly, by this hypothetical illustration I do not want to suggest that a church never needs a change in pastors. But what I do want to state, and state most emphatically, is in this hypothetical illustration what is needed is not so much a change in pastors but a radical change in the congregation! If lost people are not being won, if unreached people are not being reached, if needy people are not being helped, if the sick are not being visited—if the work of God is not being done in that place—it is the fault of and the responsibility of the people whom God has called to be His ministers!

But if such a statement were to be made in this hypothetical secret meeting, it would not be too difficult to forecast some of the objections that would be forthcoming. One objection would be something like this: "We know we have a responsibility to serve God, and we want to do our part. We want the unreached to be reached. We want the lost to be won. But we have to work for a living. That is what we are paying the pastor for, so he can give full time to do the work of God. If the work gets so large he cannot do it by himself, then we will get a minister of education. And if the work continues to grow and they cannot do it together, then we will get a minister of music. And if the work continues to grow, we will get a minister of youth. And if the work continues to grow, we will get a minister of children's work and so on. We want the work of God to be done, and we are willing to pay for it to be done." It is probable that a person would not state this viewpoint as crassly as I have, but this is precisely what we have done in practice in the life and work of our churches. Lest I be misunderstood, I am not suggesting that specialized vocational workers are not needed in our churches. A case can be made for specialized vocational workers in large churches.

However, let me give my reaction to the basic attitude that underlies the objection given. In my judgment this is the most heinous and the most irresponsible heresy that the mind of man ever perpetrated on the Word of God. A layperson cannot pay someone else to fulfill his or her ministry for God. God has called His people to the ministry, and the ministry belongs to the laity whether they know it or not. God's ministry belongs to the laity whether they fulfill it or not. And the laity is accountable unto God for the manner in which they accept and fulfill it or fail to do so.

PERSONAL LEARNING ACTIVITY 5
If laypeople were to accept and fulfill their ministry, do you think specialized vocational workers would still be needed?
List your reasons.

If laypeople were to accept and fulfill their ministry, do you think a paid ministry would still be needed? Explain.

List areas in which money would still be needed in the work of the church even if laypeople accepted and fulfilled their personal ministry.

If the emphasis on God's call of the laity to ministry were to be expressed in the hypothetical secret meeting, there is a second objection that almost certainly would be raised. Again, the deacons would state their recognition that they had some responsibility to serve God and affirm that they were willing to do their part. "But," they would say, "the pastor is the one who has been 'called' by God into the ministry. The pastor has been called to serve God fulltime. You see, we have to work for a living. We simply do not have time to do the work of God like it ought to be done. God has given the pastor a special call to fulfill God's ministry. That is the reason the pastor has primary responsibility for doing God's work in the world."

It is true that God has given the pastor a special call and a special ministry. I will speak of these in some detail in another chapter. But unequivocally it needs to be said here that this special call and special ministry is NOT to do God's ministry in the world instead of or in behalf of or for the layperson. The pastor was not called by God to be the one primarily responsible for fulfilling God's ministry of reconciliation.

What Does the Bible Say?

Since we are a Bible believing people, I am sure that long before now the question has arisen, "What does the Bible say about the doctrine of the laity?" Up to this point I have made some rather general statements, some of them, perhaps, controversial. Upon what do I base these general statements? The doctrine of the priesthood of all believers (upon which the doctrine of the laity is based) is spoken of most frequently in 1 Peter and in the Revelation. However, there is a statement from Paul that will be our first focus.

A familiar passage. There is a passage from one of Paul's letters with which we all are familiar that gives a very clear statement concerning the doctrine of the laity. The passage is found in 2 Corinthians 5:17-19: "Therefore if any man be in Christ, he is a new creature: old things are passed away; behold, all things are become new. And all things are of God, who hath reconciled us to himself by Jesus Christ, and hath given to us the ministry of reconciliation; To wit, that God was in Christ, reconciling the world unto himself, not imputing their trespasses unto them; and hath committed unto us the word of reconciliation." Every word and phrase in these verses is significant and important. However, for our purposes the focal phrase is "and hath given to us the ministry of reconciliation." Who is the *us* to whom God has given His ministry of reconciliation in the world? The answer is obvious. It refers to those who are "in Christ" to whom Paul refers in verse 17. There is no way this could refer to a select few whom God has "called" into the ministry. It refers to all Christians, and it refers to every Christian. Paul says if anyone is "in Christ" (that is, saved), this one has become a new creation by the work and grace of God; and this one is given the ministry of reconciliation. These verses also support the point made earlier that the call to salvation and the call to ministry are one and the same call. When we come to be "in Christ," we are given the ministry.

Priesthood in 1 Peter and Revelation. Two general references to all Christians as priests are made in the Book of Revelation. The first is found in Revelation 1:6: "And made us a kingdom, priests to his God and Father, to him be glory and dominion for ever and ever. Amen." (RSV). This is a part of John's salutation to those who would read this writing. As is done in a number of the New Testament letters, he is telling of the marvelous work that Christ has done for us. The latter part of verse 5 says that Christ loved us and by His blood freed us from our sins. Then in verse 6 John continues, saying that He made us a kingdom (of God's people) and also made us priests to God Himself. Here again, it is clear that the Scripture is referring to the priesthood of all believers. The second passage in Revelation is found in chapter 5, verse 10. In this chapter the question is raised, "'Who is worthy to break the seals and open the scroll?'" (Rev. 5:2, GNB). John said he "wept much" because there seemed to be no one who was worthy to open the scroll. But then, he says, "I saw a Lamb standing, as though it had been slain" (v. 6, RSV). And when this one took the scroll, "the four living creatures and the twenty-four elders fell down before the Lamb . . . and they sang a new song, saying, 'Worthy art thou to take the scroll and to open its seals, for thou wast slain and by thy blood didst ransom men for God from every tribe and tongue and people and nation, and hast made them a kingdom and priests to our God, and they shall reign on earth'" (vv. 8-10, RSV). Again, this is a general statement indicating that all of those who have been redeemed by Christ are priests before God. This is the priesthood of all believers.

The references in 1 Peter are more specific, and therefore will be more helpful in understanding the meaning of our priesthood before God. In two verses the priesthood is mentioned specifically. The first is 1 Peter 2:5, "Ye also, as lively stones, are built up a spiritual house, an holy priesthood, to offer up spiritual sacrifices, acceptable to God by Jesus Christ." The second is 1 Peter 2:9, "But ye are a

49

chosen generation, a royal priesthood, an holy nation, a peculiar people; that ye should shew forth the praises of him who hath called you out of darkness into his marvellous light."

These titles had been descriptive of old Israel (Isa. 28:16 and Ex. 19:6). Now Peter applies the titles to the church as the new Israel of God. These terms refer to all church members. There is no distinction between laity and clergy.

PERSONAL LEARNING ACTIVITY 6
List the similarities you find between 1 Peter 2:9 and God's call of Israel in Exodus 19:5-6.

A question that immediately arises is, To whom does the personal pronoun *ye* refer in verses 5 and 9 of 1 Peter 2? Verse 5 says, "Ye . . . are built up a spiritual house, an holy priesthood." Verse 9 says, "Ye are a chosen generation, a royal priesthood." Who is the *ye* to whom the writer is referring? To answer this question we have to ask another question, To whom was this letter addressed? To find the answer to this question we turn back to 1 Peter 1:1 and read: "Peter, an apostle of Jesus Christ, to the strangers scattered throughout Pontus, Galatia, Cappadocia, Asia, and Bithynia." What is translated here as, "strangers scattered throughout Pontus" in the Greek means sojourners of the dispersion of Pontus. Thus this letter was written to God's people who had experienced severe persecution and were scattered (see Acts 8:1; 11:19). The letter was not written to the elders and bishops. To go back to verses 5 and 9 of chapter 2, it is clear that the pronoun *ye* refers to the people, the laity. The writer is saying here that all of God's people are called into the priesthood.

In verse 5 it is called a "holy priesthood." Usually we think of the word *holy* as referring to moral or spiritual characteristics. If one is supposed to be holy, our usual understanding is that he or she is highly moral and virtuous. Certainly this understanding of the meaning of this word is valid. However, in the Bible, the root meaning of *holy* is to be set apart for God's use. In the Old Testament the vessels used in the temple were "holy." As an object, a vessel has no moral qualities. *Holy vessels* mean they are set apart from God's use. Thus to be a "holy priesthood" certainly means we should seek to be a highly moral people. But in a deeper way it means God has called us to be set apart for His use. The phrase which is translated *a peculiar people* in the Greek means a people of (God's) possession. We belong to God, and God has called us and set us apart for His use. This is the essence of our uniqueness as God's people (see chapter 1). We are a people called to mission.

If, then, we have been called into the priesthood, set apart by God for His use, what is our mission? In the last part of 1 Peter 2:9 the writer says we are to "shew forth the praises of him who hath called you out of darkness into his marvellous light." We are to give praises to Him who brought us out of the darkness and brokenness of sin and by His matchless grace has brought healing and light to our lives through Jesus Christ. And in giving praises to Him who healed us we will be showing forth what God can and will do for all who are in darkness and in need of the light only God can give. This is our mission because it is God's mission. He stated this same mission to Abraham in Genesis 12:3.

According to 1 Peter 2:5, the laity as God's priesthood are "to offer up spiritual sacrifices, acceptable to God by Jesus Christ." One of the functions of the priest in the Old Testament was to offer sacrifices to God in behalf of the sinful people. In the New Covenant, God's people, the laity, as a holy priesthood, are to offer "spiritual sacrifices" to God in behalf of a sinful people. Again, an important question is raised, What is the nature of the "spiritual sacrifices" which the laity are to offer to God in behalf of a sinful world? We get a clue to the answer to this question in the Book of Hebrews. In Hebrews Jesus is portrayed as the great high priest, after the order of Melchisedec (Heb. 5:6). As the high priest Jesus enters the "holy of holies" to offer His sacrifice to God in behalf of a sinful world. What is the sacrifice that Jesus offers to God? Here we have the answer to our original question, What is the nature of the "spiritual sacrifice" which we, the laity, as a holy priesthood, are to offer to God? We are to give God our lives!

An Incarnational Ministry

Today we seem to be trying to win the world to Christ primarily through the use of words. Through television, radio, and pulpit we proclaim the message of God. Throngs listen. But it seems that the throngs who listen are the people who already profess Christ as Savior or who are, at least, open to His message. Though there are exceptions, the masses in the world do not even listen to the words. This is not to say that the preached word is not powerful and effective. But it is to say that the ones who listen to the preached word, in the main, are those who are already church members. If the masses of people are ever going to hear the redeeming and reconciling message from God, it will have to come to them in another way.

This is where God's approach through incarnation comes in. Incarnation refers to the union of divinity with humanity in Jesus Christ—that is, divine God becoming a human being yet remaining divine. Humans are not incarnate beings, but as Christians we have an incarnational relationship.

If God is going to get the attention of the broken and sinful masses of the world, it will have to be done primarily through a ministry of revealing Christ through our lives and witness. If they are going to understand in any serious way the meaning of the love of God and the forgiveness of God, it will have to be done primarily through an incarnational ministry.

PERSONAL LEARNING ACTIVITY 7
What is meant by incarnational ministry? Write your understanding in one or two sentences.

What are some similarities and differences between Christ's incarnation and the Christian's incarnational ministry?

Can you give an example of an incarnational ministry?

What do I mean by an incarnational ministry? It is a ministry which a Christian with conscious intent expresses love, care, and help for a person at a point of deep need, hurt, or brokenness. Generally it is a situation in which the Christian is involved because of his or her desire to be an incarnation of the love of God to that person in that situation. Even my attempt to describe the meaning of an incarnational ministry demonstrates the difficulty of trying to communicate through the use of words. Meaning is not always clear. Understanding is limited.

So, let me become verbally incarnational and give an illustration. To see an incarnational-ministry-expressed life will make it much clearer and understandable. This hypothetical situation is based on an actual experience. Let us say that Mrs. Smith has come to understand that as a Christian she has been called by God to the ministry of the laity to be an instrument God can use to fulfill His mission of reconciliation in the world. She is very wealthy. She has a magnificent home with all the appropriate furnishings. Though she is not at all ostentatious, evidences of wealth surround her. Her deep burden and concern is for adult illiterates. She has trained to minister to those who are unable to read. She makes contact with a barber in the poor section of the city, and they make arrangements for a regular time and place for meeting. Over a period of weeks that begins to lengthen into several months, she meets with the barber, instructing him in reading. Finally, at the end of one of the sessions the barber says, "I need to ask you a question. How much do I owe you?" Mrs. Smith smiles and says, "Why, you don't owe me anything." But the barber persists: "But I want to pay you. You know that I don't have much money, but I'm grateful for what you have done for me. You have opened a whole new area of life for me. I can read a little now, and you just don't know what that means to me. This has taken a lot of time and work on your part. I want to pay you." Again Mrs. Smith smiles and says, "The fact is there is not enough money in the whole city to pay me to come down here and teach you." With a quizzical look on his face the barber replies, "I don't understand. Then why are you doing it?" Mrs. Smith says: "I'm glad you asked that. There is one who loves me and who loves you. It is because of Him that I care deeply about you. I'd like to tell you about Him." And she gave a verbal witness which is a part of this incarnational ministry. But she had no difficulty explaining to him about the love of God because he had already been the recipient of that love expressed in the life of Mrs. Smith. That is an incarnational ministry.

God got the attention of a calloused world through incarnation. Today if an unregenerate and calloused, but hurting, world is going to give attention to any word spoken about the love of God; it will be only after this love is expressed in some concrete and positive way. How can they understand the unconditional love of God unless and until they have experienced unconditional love through the ministry of a Christian? It takes the flesh and bones of a body to express this unconditional love. This is incarnational ministry.

Thus the concept that the layperson is the basic minister of God is a necessity from both a biblical and a practical perspective. Biblically the doctrine of the priesthood of all believers teaches that God has called His people—all His people—to be His ministers. From a practical perspective it is a physical impossibility for the pastor and other staff to be in all the places of brokenness where God wants to minister. There simply are not enough of them. They cannot be in all the executive offices where difficult but important decisions are made that affect multitudes of people. They cannot be in all the shops and stores. They cannot be in all the factories. They cannot be in all the hospitals. They cannot be in all the homes where there is hurt. They cannot be in all the places in the ghetto where brokenness runs rife.

But God's people are in these places. From early Monday morning through late Friday afternoon, over the weekends, and in night shifts, Christians are in all these places. Too often the problem is they are just being good people but are not being ministers. And a second problem occurs when Christians of many years do not know how to be ministers. And so the work of God languishes because the people whom God has called to be His basic ministers have not adequately understood their call; they have not adequately accepted it, and therefore are not adequately fulfilling it.

Numerous questions continue to arise. If the layperson is the basic minister, what is the task of the pastor? If God calls the laity to fulfill His mission in the world, what is involved in that mission? How do we do it? These are questions for the following chapters.

CHAPTER 4

THE NATURE
MISSION

OF GOD'S
AND OURS

CHAPTER 4

THE NATURE OF GOD'S MISSION AND OURS

If, as I have said, God calls His people to mission, a question immediately arises. What is the nature of the mission to which God has called us? Of what does it consist? What is involved in expressing it? It becomes a matter of prime importance for us to seek to understand with clarity what is involved in this mission in order that we might know what we must do to fulfill it. As God's people we need to make sure that we are neither mistaken nor limited in our understanding of the mission to which we are called. It may be that we are doing one thing when, in fact, God has called us to do something else. Or, it may be that we are fulfilling a part of God's mission but are failing to carry out another important aspect of His mission. What is God's mission in the world which He has called us to fulfill?

Personal Salvation

Throughout our history Southern Baptists have emphasized the necessity and the importance of each individual having a personal, saving relationship with Jesus Christ. We have to confess with shame that as a general rule our personal efforts have not matched our theology, but as a denomination our efforts have been far from failure.

The nature of humans. Why has this emphasis on personal salvation been so central in our theology and emphasis? The witness of the Bible is that humans are sinners. "For all have sinned, and come short of the glory of God" (Rom. 3:23). This sin is not minor wrongdoings. It is of a most serious nature, reaching to the very center of our being and because of it we are "by nature the children of wrath" (Eph. 2:3). Because of sin humans are alienated from God, and "the wages of sin is death" (Rom. 6:23).

There is a tendency on the part of some religious thinkers to minimize the fact of sin. They sometimes refuse to use the term; or when they do, they use it only most reluctantly, preferring rather to speak of "mistakes," "maladjustments," or "societal gaps." This is a far cry from the biblical view of humans. In the Bible there is no rosy view of the nature of humans. There is no humanistic doctrine of a human's innate self-sufficiency. The Bible treats the human predicament with utmost seriousness. Sin is personal. Sin is against God. Humanity is responsible. As George Forell says: "All human troubles stem from this one source. None can be solved ultimately unless the relationship to God, broken through sin, is restored."[1]

Disorder, not order, is at the center of a person's life. Certainly we need to help change a person's environment. Certainly we need to help provide for him or her the best social, economic, and emotional setting possible in which to live. But doing this will not solve all of a person's problems. All of us have problems within—of a specifically personal and spiritual nature—which must be solved.

Basic human nature has not changed in the last two thousand years. With all our technological and scientific progress, we are essentially the same as people were in the first century. This time in our lives is not called the "Age of Anxiety" or the "Era of the Aspirin" for nothing. Something is still wrong—seriously wrong—with modern human beings. The question is, Can this something be dealt with or eradicated by man's own efforts—education, technology, psychology, or social progress? Evidence points otherwise. In every area of life—in government, in multinational corporations, in small businesses, in social relations—we see inhumanity to one another; we see graft and greed. The most educated and the least educated, the richest and the poorest are still plagued with the problem of sin. The greatest scientists, through science alone, have not eradicated the problem. The present situation affirms the biblical perspective, all humans are sinners. We need personal salvation.

God's action in Christ. The reality of sin in human experience is of such radical nature that people, in their own strength, are inadequate to deal with it. The remedy must come from God. According to Alexander Miller,[2] "sin is terrible and redemption is costly." Alienation from God is so deep and so severe that the solution to people's problems cannot be found either in reason or in progress. Miller points out the fact that scientific progress has dispelled many of the ghosts that plagued religious humankind at an earlier age of history. This seems encouraging until we pause and consider that "men now fear the scientists more than they feared the ghosts." However, one who has an understanding of the biblical faith should not expect reason to be the ultimate solution to people's problems. In biblical faith nature, reason, and history are all perverted by a most radical distortion." Humans are gripped in a tetanus-like death. "The self turns in upon the self" and thus contributes to his or her own self-destruction. He can be freed from this deathly cycle "only by the injection of some serum" which comes from outside of oneself. Redemption cannot come through reason because the egocentricity with which persons are afflicted "perverts all reason." Humanity cannot find deliverance through an act of its own will because its will "is intrinsically self-will." This is the essence of humankind's problem, not the source of his solution. "There is no stance in the human psyche from which an attack can be leveled against this radical distemper, since the distemper poisons the whole self." This is why the Bible "calls not for a resolve but for a rescue." This is why, when the Bible speaks of humankind's fundamental problem, it speaks "not of progress but of the coming of a Messiah."

God, in infinite love, has acted in behalf of humankind. People's need is radical, and God's solution is radical. He gave His Son. The pivotal verse here is one which because of its familiarity too often fails to have anything like the significance for us it should have. "For God so loved the world, that he gave his only begotten Son, that whosoever believeth in him should not perish, but have everlasting life" (John 3:16). Paul said, "God was in Christ, reconciling the world to himself" (2 Cor. 5:19). He who knew no sin bore our sins "in his own body" (1 Pet. 2:24). Concerning His own mission Jesus said: "The Son of man came not to be ministered unto, but to minister, and to give his life a ransom for many" (Mark 10:45).

People must become "new." This re-creation, however, cannot come from within; it must come from outside—from Him who created humankind in the first place. As Jesus said in His conversation with Nicodemus, a person must "be born again" (or be born from above) (John 3:3). Or as Paul said, he must become a "new creation" (2 Cor. 5:17, RSV). It is this work of God that gives persons a new meaning for life, a new center for life, a new motivation for life, and a new direction for life.

PERSONAL LEARNING ACTIVITY 8

Do you feel that the pastor and church staff members have a greater responsibility for engaging in personal evangelism than does a layperson? Why or why not?

List some of the reasons why you think a layperson does not engage more in personal evangelism.

Jesus' Ministry

If there was one group of people who received the special focus of Jesus, it was the sick, the poor, and the oppressed—those on the bottom end of the socioeconomic ladder. This should come as no surprise to us, because this was the focus of God throughout the Old Testament. So many of God's teachings remind His people how they are to care for and minister to those whom life has hurt. "When thou gatherest the grapes of thy vineyard, thou shalt not glean it afterward: it shall be for the stranger, for the fatherless, and for the widow" (Deut. 24:21). This emphasis was continued in the New Testament. John the Baptist in his preaching, like the prophets of old, spoke a stern and severe message to the people. He called them a "generation of vipers" (Luke 3:7). He warned them not to depend on any shallow, external relationship as evidence that they were in a right relationship with God—"begin not to say within yourselves, We have Abraham to our father" (v. 8). He called on them to repent and to "bring forth . . . fruits worthy of repentance" (v. 8). When the people asked what they should do, one expression of their repentance was, "He that hath two coats, let him impart to him that hath none; and he that hath meat, let him do likewise" (v. 11).

Jesus was a person-centered teacher. Jesus taught in and through life experience. But in these teachings, the plight of the outcast and the needy, as well as the lost, was a central focus. In His first sermon in His hometown, Nazareth, He selected as His text the passage from Isaiah: "The Spirit of the Lord is upon me, because he hath anointed me to preach the gospel to the poor; he hath sent me to heal the broken-hearted, to preach deliverance to the captives, and recovering of sight to the blind, to set at liberty them that are bruised, to preach the acceptable year of the Lord" (Luke 4:18-19).

The entire life and ministry of Jesus demonstrates Jesus' concern for persons in their human hurts, as well as His concern for people finding salvation through a personal relationship with God. However, the parable of the judgment is pivotal in teaching that the people who claim to be God's people must be concerned about people in their human hurts.

A. T. Robertson, great Southern Baptist Greek scholar, called Matthew 25 "The Great Eschatological Discourse" (teachings concerning last things). Matthew says: "When the Son of man shall come in his glory, and all the holy angels with him, then shall he sit upon the throne of his glory: and before him shall be gathered all the nations: and he shall separate them one from another, as a shepherd divideth his sheep from the goats: and he shall set the sheep on his right hand, but the goats on the left. Then shall the King say unto them on his right hand, Come, ye blessed of my Father, inherit the kingdom prepared for you from the foundation of the world."

Jesus then indicated the kinds of things that had been characteristic of the life of those who "inherit the kingdom." He continued the parable telling of those who do not inherit the kingdom. "Then shall he say also unto them on the left hand, Depart from me, ye cursed, into everlasting fire, prepared for the devil and his angels: for I was an hungred, and ye gave me no meat: I was thirsty, and ye gave me no drink: I was a stranger, and ye took me not in: naked, and ye clothed me not: sick, and in prison, and ye visited me not." When the listeners protested and asked when they had seen the Lord in these kinds of circumstances, His reply was, "Verily I say unto you, Inasmuch as ye did it not to one of the least of these, ye did it not to me." His concluding words were, "And these shall go away into everlasting punishment: but the righteous into life eternal" (Matt. 25:31-46).

Everything that God has to say about any major topic or issue cannot be said in one verse or one parable or even in one section. Therefore, the total Bible has to be used to determine the biblical teaching concerning any major area. But in this one parable the major evidence that one belongs to God is how one treats the hungry, the thirsty, the stranger, the naked, and those in prison, that is, those who are on the lowest socioeconomic scale in society.

Social Involvement

Personal salvation is central in the mission in which God is engaged in the world and to which He has called His people. Social involvement is also a necessary aspect of God's eternal redemptive mission. Undoubtedly, there would be universal agreement among Southern Baptists concerning the necessity of personal salvation as a necessary part of God's mission, but there is not universal agreement about the necessity of social awareness and concern. During the last few years there has been a strong swing among conservatives and evangelicals to embrace social concerns and involvement. But there are earnest, sincere, and dedicated Christians who feel deeply that God is concerned only with solving the spiritual problems of man.

Objections to social involvement. Without any attempt to be exhaustive, note some of the objections these friends have to a social emphasis in the life and work of our churches.

One of the main reasons for the rejection of a social emphasis was a fear of and negative reaction to what was called "the social gospel." By "social gospel" these people meant a "gospel" that denied the sinfulness (or lostness) of man and also denied that salvation was through Christ alone. This fear grew in the latter part of the last century and the early part of this century. It was in reaction to certain developments that took place in certain religious groups. During this period certain religious groups began to develop what conservatives call a liberal theology.

These groups said that a salvation experience during one's mature years, which was the norm in the 1800's, was not the only way one could be saved. In fact, they said it was not the normal way for a person to be saved. This view, they said, did not make an adequate place in the kingdom of God for the young child. Based on the way some groups interpreted the biblical emphasis on the covenant, this view held that emotional conversion experience was not necessary; rather, a child could be "nurtured" into the kingdom of God. That is, based on this covenant theology, a child, with proper training at home and in the church, could grow into the kingdom without having a traditional conversion experience. Horace Bushnell, one of the fathers of the liberal movement in theology, held as his basic thesis "that the child is to grow up a Christian, and need never know himself as being otherwise."[3] Those who were conservative in their theology and evangelistic in their approach thought these "liberals" had rejected the sinfulness of man and that salvation was possible only through a personal experience with Jesus Christ.

The religious groups who held this "liberal theology" also became involved with the social ills that were prevalent at that time. Those who were conservative came to identify "liberal theology" and social involvement. Because they rejected the liberal theology, they also rejected the social involvement. Also the conservatives accused the liberals of holding the position that all one needed to be saved was to have one's social needs met.

There was both truth and error in this interpretation by the conservatives. Undoubtedly, there were those who held and practiced precisely what the conservatives said. On the other hand, Walter Rauschenbusch, the chief apostle of the "social gospel" movement, emphasized the necessity of individual, personal salvation. He recognized that each person is a sinner and "the salvation of the individual is . . . . an essential part of salvation." He said, "Every new being is a new problem of salvation . . . our discussion can not pass personal salvation by."[4]

Nevertheless, those who were conservative in their theology and who held to the necessity of a "new birth" experience, rejected firmly any emphasis on social involvement by their churches.

Also, the advocates of this position point out that today many institutions (government, social agencies, and so on) care for and minister to the human needs of people, but God has ordained only one institution and entrusted to it His message of divine redemption—the church. Therefore, our churches must focus on one God-given task, namely, the personal salvation of lost people. Many of these people point out that they are in favor of having the human needs of people met; but if the churches turn aside from the task, if the churches go off on a tangent, there is no other institution in all the world that can or will minister to people in terms of their basic spiritual needs.

Social involvement, a necessary part of God's mission. Social involvement is an integral part of God's mission, and therefore it is a necessary part of the ministry of our churches. Those who support this point of view often point out that those who make a great distinction between soul and body tend to follow Greek philosophy in their view of persons rather than a biblical view. Greek philosophy, following Plato and Aristotle, held that a person is a dualism: soul and body, spirit and matter. Matter, the physical, was the lower part of a person which he or she held in common with all other animals. The goal of the person was to move upward to develop the form or spirit which made him or her to be a unique human being.

The Bible, on the other hand, rejects this dualism and speaks of person as being a unity. Genesis 2:7 says, "The Lord God formed man of the dust of the ground, and breathed into his nostrils the breath of life; and man became a living soul." The individual in his or her essential being is a unity. The person is a "living soul." Thus, in the biblical view there is not the great difference between the soul and the body. The physical and the spiritual are fused in a living soul. Throughout the Old Testament in God's teaching of His people, there is a major and recurring emphasis on the care of the poor, the widows, the orphans, and the stranger that is within your gate. This emphasis, of course, continues in the New Testament.

PERSONAL LEARNING ACTIVITY 9
Having read the arguments in support of the churches becoming involved in the human-social needs of people, what other points favoring this position would you add?

You have considered two views—(1) God's mission and therefore the church's mission is limited to the spiritual-personal salvation and (2) God's mission, and therefore the church's mission, includes both personal salvation and social involvement. Which do you feel is the biblical position regarding this question?

What, for you, are the decisive arguments? State briefly.

Two Emphases in Balance

One of the reasons Southern Baptists have emphasized personal salvation and tended to minimize social involvement was based on a theological perspective. In the latter part of the last century and the early part of this century, a rather large segment of Protestantism began to emphasize nurture as the normal mode by which individuals entered the kingdom of God rather than through a conversion experience. Other issues were also involved, but this was one of the key issues. Southern Baptists rejected this "liberal" theology. About this same time these same churches also began a rather vigorous ministry to the social needs of the poor and outcast. Southern Baptists tended to identify this social ministry with the liberal theology.

Because they rejected the liberal theology, they also rejected the social concern.

We do not need anything to interfere with personal salvation. We do not need less emphasis in this area; we need more. Therefore, this practical reason raises a very important question. Would raising our consciousness of and involvement in meeting the human and social needs of people lessen our involvement in personal evangelism? Can the church carry personal salvation and social involvement in balance in its life and ministry? Will one be neglected? Can the church do both? I say we must, because this is what God calls for His people, the church, to do. This is our challenge. This is our opportunity.

Is there any evidence that these two emphases can both be carried out in balance? There certainly is evidence that this balance was in the life and ministry of Jesus. Likewise there is evidence that this balance was done in the life of the early church. "But," someone may ask, "is there any more recent evidence than that?" As indicated earlier, at the beginning of this century a large segment of Protestantism rejected the conversion approach to salvation. Also these religious denominations became deeply committed to social ministry in the life of their churches. Southern Baptists were involved in some social issues but not the same ones as the social gospel advocates. Southern Baptists put great emphasis on evangelism. So in this century the groups who emphasized social involvement de-emphasized evangelism, and the groups who emphasized evangelism de-emphasized social involvement. For this reason it is necessary for us to go back to the 1800's to get a more recent answer to the question. Can the churches emphasize both evangelism and social involvement and not neglect either?

The evangelists and the revival period between about 1830 and 1865 illustrate the fact that the answer to this question is affirmative. Timothy L. Smith in an excellent book, *Revivalism and Social Reform,* called attention to a fact that has been lost or forgotten, namely, during the revivals of the mid-1800's the evangelists were among the leaders in social reform. The loss of this knowledge has been tragic both for evangelical religion and for society. According to Smith, "Liberalism on social issues, not reaction, was the dominant note which evangelical preachers sounded before 1860. The most influential of them, from Albert Barnes and Samuel S. Schmucker to Edward Norris Kirk and Matthew Simpson, defined carefully the relationship between personal salvation and community improvement."[5] As early as 1835, Edward Beecher wrote that the task of

Christians was "not merely to preach the gospel to every creature, but to reorganize human society in accordance with the law of God. To abolish all corruptions in religion and all abuses in the social system and, so far as it has been erected on false principles, to take it down and erect it anew."[6]

There were, of course, reform movements and influences of a non-religious type during this period. But, according to Charles Cole, the religious reformers were primarily responsible for bringing about social changes. In the fight against poverty, delinquency, and other evils, and in the fight for temperance, women's rights, and antislavery, "those standing on the rock of piety"[7] brought about these changes. The Salvation Army emerged out of the revival of 1858-59. Throughout the years this group has demonstrated both a fervent evangelistic witness and a concern for persons in their social needs.

There is also evidence that in addition to meeting the human needs of individuals, the evangelists were deeply involved in seeking to change the laws and structures of society that permitted human exploitation. Those today who say that the only task of the minister is to "preach the gospel" would not have found support among the evangelists of the mid-nineteenth century. Henry Ward Beecher said, "It is the duty of the minister of the Gospel to preach on every side of political life. I do not say that he may. I say that he must."[8]

Since slavery was the burning issue of the time, this was naturally a matter of major concern for the evangelists. Joshua Leavitt, head of *The Evangelist* in the 1830's, greatly popularized the abolitionist cause through his writings. George B. Cheever, a revered evangelist with deep concern for and commitment to personal evangelism, became deeply involved in numerous social concerns including slavery. To go back another century in time to England, we find John Wesley, one of the all time great evangelists, vigorously condemning slavery in every form. So deep were his feelings that the last letter Wesley wrote, just six days before his death, was addressed to William Wilberforce to encourage his continued violent opposition to slavery both in England and in America.

The evangelists were also deeply concerned about the plight of the poor. The depth of Wesley's personal concern is demonstrated in one of his letters. "I have two silver spoons at London and two at Bristol. This is all the plate I have at present, and I shall not buy more while so many around me want bread."[9] In additon he also encouraged his followers not only to share their clothing with the poor but also to employ the women who were out of work to do sewing. They should be paid the "going wage" for their work and then given further assistance according to their need. Again in his *Journal,* speaking of the poor, Wesley wrote, "I visited as many more as I could. I found some in their cells underground; others in their garrets, half starved both with cold and hunger, added to weakness and pain. But I found not one of them unemployed who was able to crawl about the room. So wickedly, devilishly false is that common objection, 'They are poor only because they are idle.' "[10]

In Wesley's preface to his 1739 *Hymn Book* he wrote, "The Gospel of Christ knows no religion but social, no holiness, but social holiness."[11] Bready concludes that "Wesley . . . was a mighty social reformer; for by initiating . . . a marvelous spiritual movement latent with moral imperatives, he opened the springs of human sympathy and understanding, which in turn inspired and nourished a glorious succession of social reforms."[12]

What these evangelists did was not perfect, nor am I setting them up as models. They made mistakes as all humans do. I am simply pointing out that here were men deeply committed to social concern and social involvement. This is practical evidence that it is possible for God's people to emphasize both personal salvation and social involvement and keep both of them in balance. Not only is it possible, but in my opinion it is imperative that we do so in order to be faithful to the whole gospel.

PERSONAL LEARNING ACTIVITY 10
Do you believe that it is both desirable and possible for a church to emphasize both personal salvation and social involvement and keep both in proper balance? Indicate what you think is the strongest argument that supports your view.

On the scale from 1 to 10, indicate the depth of your feeling about this point.
1   2   3   4   5   6   7   8   9   10

The Challenge

Jesus gave the pattern to follow. He was vitally concerned about a person's spiritual relationship with God and that person's physical and mental well-being. The challenge then is to be like Him. His was not an "either/or" ministry but a "both/and" ministry.

Jesus ministered in various ways. To the sick He gave physical and spiritual healing. To the outcast He gave emotional and spiritual hope. To the hungry He gave physical and spiritual food. Following His pattern means that believers will minister in various ways.

The challenge of Christ is to meet needs of people where they are. It may be providing food to a needy family. If this is done in the name of Christ then physical and spiritual needs are considered. It may be listening to an abused wife tell her heart-aching story. By offering advice, shelter, and prayer on her behalf, emotional, physical, and spiritual ministry takes place.

The believer, of course, wants others to come to a saving relationship in Christ. But the believer's ministry does not end there. The believer will continue to meet needs by involving a new convert in the life of the church. The believer's ministry does not end with church involvement either. The new convert will receive constant encouragement to live for Christ at home, on the job, and other places.

Evangelism, mission involvement, teaching, training, and social involvement were aspects of Jesus' life and ministry. He challenges the believer to follow the model of His life and get involved with the total person—physical, mental, social, emotional, and spiritual. This is the mission of God and the mission of the church.

Again questions flood our minds. If this is God's mission and the church's mission, who are the basic ministers of this mission? It is to this question we turn in chapter 5.

Notes

[1]George Wolfgang Forell, *The Protestant Faith* (Philadelphia: Fortress Press, 1960), p. 137.

[2]Alexander Miller, *The Renewal of Man* (Garden City, NY: Doubleday & Co., 1955), pp. 56-59.

[3]Horace Bushnell, *Christian Nurture* (New York: Charles Scribner's Sons, 1916), p. 4.

[4]Walter Rauschenbusch, *A Theology for the Social Gospel* (New York: Macmillan, 1917), pp. 95-96.

[5]Timothy L. Smith, *Revivalism and Social Reform* (New York: Abingdon, 1957), p. 151.

[6]Ibid., p. 225.

[7]Charles C. Cole, Jr., *The Social Ideas of the Northern Evangelists, 1826-1860* (New York: Columbia University Press, 1954), p. 97.

[8]Ibid., p. 132.

[9]J. Wesley Bready, *England Before and After Wesley* (New York: Harper & Brother, n.d.), p. 238.

[10]Percy Livingston Parker, ed., *The Heart of John Wesley's Journal* (London: Fleming H. Revell Co., n.d.), p. 206.

[11]Bready, *England Before and After Wesley*, p. 297.

[12]Ibid., p. 252.

CHAPTER 5

THE PASTOR

LAITY

AS EQUIPPER

THE PASTOR AS EQUIPPER

If it is true that God called His people to a mission when He called them to be His people and if it is true that he called each Christian to be a minister of that mission of reconciliation (2 Cor. 5:17-18), to what is the pastor called?

If the layperson is responsible for fulfilling God's ministry in the world, what is the pastor supposed to do? Some may ask, if the laity are called to be the basic ministers, do we even need a pastor? The answer to that question is a resounding YES! The work of the pastor is both a biblical and a practical necessity. On the other hand some may say: "I always thought the pastor was the one who was called to the ministry. I thought the pastor was called in a special way to do the ministry. Now I am being told that the laity are the ones who are responsible for doing the ministry. I'm getting confused." Two questions need to be asked about this statement. First, is the pastor called to "the ministry" or called to "a ministry"? Second, is the pastor called "to do the ministry"? To respond briefly to both questions, the pastor is called to a high, a holy, a significant, a pivotal ministry. The pastor is called to a special ministry. But the one who serves a church as pastor is not called to the ministry any more than any other layperson. Neither is the pastor called to do the ministry any more than any other layperson. What, then is the calling, the ministry, the task of the pastor? It is to this important question to which we now turn our attention.

A Brief Biblical View

As professor of Christian Education in one of our seminaries, I had been working for years with workers in Sunday School, Church Training, and missionary education through Woman's Missionary Union and Baptist Men's work. I had taught courses in leadership enlistment and development. I had written two books on teaching. So I was obviously aware that laypeople had an important responsibility to serve God. But the idea that the laity, not the pastor, had the primary responsibility to fulfill God's ministry was revolutionary for me. When I contemplated sharing this idea and its implications with others through sermons, conferences, and articles, I thought the response of pastors would be one of overwhelming joy and affirmation. At last, they would be able to get out from under the impossible load of responsibility which they carried. I thought it would be the laity who would tend to be negative in their response. But, to my surprise the laity, at least a nucleus of the laity, were positive in their response.

However, there were pastors who either had some serious reservations or were definitely opposed to this emphasis on the ministry of the laity. I need also to state that there were those among the laity who also were either disinterested or opposed but for reasons that were different from those of the pastor. These pastors generally had no problem with the emphasis that was being given to the laity as responsible for God's ministry. Rather their difficulty was with the emphasis that was given to the role of the pastor. They felt that "Something was being taken from them and their calling." As someone has said, these pastors felt in emphasizing the equal responsibility of laity and pastors for fulfilling God's ministry in the world, they (the pastors) were being "pulled down" from the high and holy calling they had received from God. This reaction was not made in an arrogant spirit. Many of these pastors had surrendered to fulfill the ministry of the One who "called us with an holy calling" (2 Tim. 1:9) only after a period of great struggle. There is an intensity surrounding this call similar to that expressed by Paul when he said: "Woe is unto me, if I preach not the gospel" (1 Cor. 9:16). Though there is an awareness that the task to which they are called is overwhelming and often they cry, "Who is sufficient for these things?" (2 Cor. 2:16), yet they also cry, "Thanks be to God, who in Christ always leads us in triumph" (2 Cor. 2:14, RSV). I understand this sense of call because it was precisely my sense of call from God.

However, I am now becoming aware that a part of my understanding of God's call in my life was partially determined by the religious tradition in which I grew up rather than by biblical understanding. For example, it is quite clear that the phrase I quoted above ("called us with an holy calling," 2 Tim. 1:9) does not refer to Paul's special calling as a preacher (as I had always thought) but rather refers to his (Paul's) and Timothy's (and all of God's people) call to salvation. Thus the above use of this Scripture to refer to the call to be a preacher was, in fact, a misuse of Scripture. The latter part of verse 9 says that this calling was not on the basis of our works (salvation is not of works) but was on the basis of His purpose (His call to mission) and on the basis of His grace (salvation is gift). In verse 11 Paul speaks of his appointment as "a preacher and apostle and a teacher."

It must be admitted that to ascertain the nature of the calling, the role, the responsibility, the authority of those called to leadership roles in the early church is exceedingly complex and difficult. It is difficult first of all because of limited sources. The writers of the New Testament evidently were more concerned with the quality of the life and spiritual functioning of the churches than with the organizational structure. Thus in their writings they deal more with the spiritual quality of life of the churches than with organizational leadership. In those relatively few places where leadership roles are discussed, the writers go into far more detail concerning the quality of life of these leaders than with their organizational relationships (1 Tim. 3:1-13).

The Task of the Pastor

What is the work of the pastor? Let's answer the question first of all by saying what he is not called to do. The pastor is not called to be the one primarily responsible for *doing* the ministry in the place of others. The designation of pastor connotes that he will guide in the work of ministry. The pastor has a ministry just as every believer has a ministry.

According to the Scriptures the pastor is to preach (Acts 15:32), to oversee (1 Tim. 3:1), to shepherd (1 Pet. 5:2-3), to evangelize (2 Tim. 4:5), and to rule/preside (1 Tim. 5:17). All of these designations point to one central task. The pastor is to help the believers grow into mature Christians who will minister according to their calling.

The classical statement of the pastor's task is found in Ephesians 4:11-12. The King James Version translates this, "And he gave some, apostles; and some, prophets; and some, evangelists; and some, pastors and teachers; For the perfecting of the saints, for the work of the ministry, for the edifying of the body of Christ." There are three parallel clauses here that seemingly indicate the work the pastor is to do—perfect the saints, do the work of the ministry, and edify the body of Christ.

Translators of the King James Version inserted the commas to separate these three clauses. In the original Greek manuscripts there were no punctuation marks. Some contemporary versions do not insert the first comma. Without the comma it is clear that there are not three separate functions of the pastor in relationship to equipping the believers. These contemporary translations give a better interpretation of verse 12:

His gifts were made that Christians might be properly equipped for their service, that the whole body might be built up. (Phillips)

In order to get His holy people ready to serve as workers and build the body of Christ. (Beck)

For the immediate equipment of God's people for the work of service, for the ultimate building up of the body of Christ. (Williams)

To prepare God's people for works of service, so that the body of Christ may be built up. (NIV)

For the equipping of the saints for the work of service, to the building up of the body of Christ. (NASB)

Here is my personal free translation of the verses—"He gave some to be apostles, some to be prophets, some to be evangelists, and some to be pastor-teachers to equip God's people for their ministry and in this way the body of Christ is to be built up." Thus, from a biblical perspective, the central task of the pastor is very clear. The pastor is to help those who are believers to grow and develop toward maturity and to equip them in their ministry of fulfilling God's mission in the world.

Many pastors have done a great deal in equipping the saints. These concerned pastors have provided avenues for members to develop and mature. It is a tragedy that large numbers of church members have not taken advantage of the equipping that is being offered.

What is the answer? How can we get more people to take advantage of training opportunities? How can the pastor be helped to help his church members? Here are four suggested areas of consideration in which changes may need to take place.

Bring focus to ministry. At the present time church members too often expect the pastor to do an impossible task. He is to be an administrator, an evangelist, a preacher, a pastor, a teacher, a counselor, an organizer, a promoter, a scholar, and other things. Dedicated pastors try to fulfill all of these expectations.

A study was made several years ago of the major responsibilities of the pastor. It concluded that the average pastor spent most of his working time doing administrative tasks. However, most pastors did not enjoy doing administration; and they did not do it well. Is this typical in our churches today?

Administration is important. The church is an institution and needs to be administered in the most effective way possible. We need organizations in the church for the orderly and effective functioning of God's work. These organizations need to be administered. The central calling and task of the pastor is not to do the detail work of the organizations but to equip members so that the work will be done. When a pastor gets caught up in doing the detail work too much himself, there is no time or energy left for training others.

When a pastor emphasizes his administrative responsibilities over his equipping responsibilities, the church may grow as an institution. But there will be lackings in the spiritual depth of the members because they have not been equipped for ministry.

A focus on ministry is essential. At the present time too many pastors are expected to do many things to keep the church functioning. All these things are good and need to be done. But if the pastor is to focus on ministry, how will this administration get done? A possible answer is to let the laity fulfill the responsibility based on their gifts. Many church members are better equipped to do the detail work in the organization of the church than the pastor. Then the pastor would be freed up to focus on the ministry best suited to his gifts.

The focus of the pastor's ministry must be on the caring, developing, maturing, and equipping of God's people to be the ministers for fulfilling God's mission in the world. In the most deeply experiential manner, the pastor must come to understand and internalize his call to equip those in his charge. If those in his charge are growing, maturing, becoming equipped, and are fulfilling their ministry of God's reconciliation in the world, then the pastor is fulfilling his calling.

To make this focus on ministry a reality, many pastors must make a change in what they have emphasized in the past. It will not be easy.

Role expectations by members. The pastor is not the only one who must make a change. A change in attitude must come from members as well. At the present time there are certain roles most church members expect the pastor to fill. Many of these roles are based on tradition and not on Scripture. There may be those who say the pastor has a special call "to the ministry." What they mean by this statement is that the preacher is supposed to *do the ministry* in a way that a layperson is not. Examples of this attitude: A layperson may choose to visit or not visit; the pastor *must* visit. A layperson may choose to witness or not witness; the pastor *must* witness. Hospital visitation is a must for the pastor, but not for the layperson.

The role expectations of the church members is a powerful force in shaping the ministry of many pastors. Just as peer pressure among teenagers is a molding force of life-style, so is member expectation of pastors a molding force of their ministry.

What is the answer? A solution lies in a proper attitude toward commitment to seek equipping.

Commitment to seek equipping. Church members must be willing to accept the biblical role of the pastor as an equipper. They must be willing to avail themselves of his guidance in finding their gifts and places of service. Unfortunately there are large numbers in our churches who do not avail themselves of the opportunities for growth and development. These unfortunate members are not a part of regular programs of Bible study, discipleship training, mission study, and other opportunities for growth. Some who do attend come so sporadically that no serious learning or equipping can take place. Too many of the church membership see the area of growth and development as optional in their Christian lives. They have not learned that training in the Christian life is not optional.

A typical person who fits this category of an unfortunate church member has gone only part of the way in the Christian life. He has made a profession of faith. He has been baptized and united with the church. He has received salvation, the forgiveness of sin, and eternal life. But by his actions he is not growing and developing into a useful citizen of God's kingdom on earth. His actions speak loud and say, "This is all I want. I just want to go to heaven when I die. I really do not care for the other part of religion."

A crucial question arises. Does one who is truly a Christian have the option of selecting one part of the Christian faith and rejecting another part? Being saved is more than just getting into heaven. Salvation is a continuing process involving growth in the Christian life. Growth comes about as the believer is equipped and uses his/her gifts for ministry. One shows the world that salvation is taking place by the way gifts are used.

The believer must seek to be equipped. As a "babe in Christ" a new believer has a longing to share what has happened to him/her. This spontaneous and fervent witnessing is a beautiful sign that genuine salvation is taking place. At some point the new believer will begin to realize that he/she needs to be equipped to function according to God's expectations. The Christian will begin to seek ways of strengthening his/her call to ministry.

When God calls us to salvation, He calls us to ministry. Just as the pastor has a call, so does every Christian have a call. Whatever field or endeavor that call may lead us to, it is just as genuine as that of those who preach, teach, evangelize, rule, oversee, and shepherd.

I have known both men and women who experienced what we call "a call to ministry." These were going to enter a religious vocation. They had such deep commitment to this call that, at great sacrifice, they did everything necessary to seek and get the teaching and training they needed "for the ministry." Many times without money, sometimes without financial support from home, sometimes already married and with a family, they were willing to pay the price of doing without necessities to get their training in college and seminary.

Every Christian should have this depth of commitment to a call. If every believer yearned to develop his/her ministry the way some have who are "entering the ministry," the church would go through such a change that every part of the globe would feel the impact.

Approach to training. Another change I suggest with regard to our growing, developing, equipping task is that we expand the approaches we use in teaching. Over the years I have observed the teaching that has been done in our churches, particularly in our Sunday Schools. It seems that we have tended to use, almost exclusively, the devotional approach. In this approach the teacher is concerned with bringing out the truths in the verses being studied. These truths are presented and studied in such a way that the members are encouraged to believe and accept. There is the hope that the truths will be incorporated into the lives of the members. This approach to teaching is good and helpful. I am not suggesting that we do away with this approach. We just need to use other approaches along with this one. The devotional approach, if used exclusively, does not allow the teacher to open up areas of needs class members may be sensing.

The devotional approach generally emphasizes the feeling aspect of a member's experiences. Factual knowledge in this approach many times is insufficient as a foundation for learning at a higher level. Granted that factual knowledge is not the highest type of learning needed in the Christian faith. On the other hand, there would be few who would not confess that we as Christians need a more mature knowledge of Holy Scripture.

Neither does the devotional approach train people in the how-to involved in performing certain activities or tasks. Training people in how to do certain things is not a goal of the devotional approach in teaching. Yet, for many Christians, it is in the realm of how-to that we are woefully weak. The point I am making is that the devotional approach is not the best approach in teaching the how-to skills of the Christian life.

The devotional approach to teaching has its place. It emphasizes and contributes to the personal aspect of religion. This emphasis is important. A personal relationship with God through Christ is fundamental in our Christian experience and growth.

The almost exclusive use of this approach has been one factor that has led to the personal aspect becoming the dominant aspect in our understanding and expression of the Christian faith. One evidence of this is seen in many of the songs we sing. Look through the titles and verses of hymns used in your church. Note the large number of songs that major on what God has done for us and how that affects our personal relationship with Him. This personal relationship emphasis is important and necessary, even basic.

My point is that the devotional aspect is only a part of our total relationship with God. The more practical aspect that deals with the how-to's of functioning in God's will is a part of that relationship also.

The doctrine of the laity recognizes and emphasizes the centrality of one's personal relationship with God as being foundational. The doctrine places equal emphasis on what God calls us to do for Him. To major only on what God has done for us is to negate the second part of the covenant relationship. That is what we have been called to do for Him. This emphasis on only one part of the God-humankind relationship was Israel's problem. The Israelites accepted what God had said He would do for them, but they failed to understand what God had called them to do for Him. To what extent have present-day Christians been guilty of this same mistake?

The devotional approach to teaching has developed the personal feeling aspect of our faith, but it has left us weak in applying our ministerial calling. Too many Christians have missed out on the basic knowledge of knowing what to do as God's ministers. They may feel good in situations requiring only heart-felt religion, but they may feel inadequate when it comes to applying learned skills in ministry.

Many times a pastor has heard "I don't know how" when he has sought to enlist someone in service. The tragedy is that the statement is true. Too many church members do not know how to do the work of God inside and outside the church. They may have a "I want to" feeling but recognize they do not have the know-how.

This lack of know-how points up most emphatically that the devotional approach to teaching has been used to a far greater degree than

81

the application approach. A change is necessary in our approaches to teaching. There must be a balance between the devotional approach and the skill development/application approach.

PERSONAL LEARNING ACTIVITY 11
Which of these four suggested changes affects you most? In what way? Why?

Which of these four changes affects you least? Why?

What are some practical suggestions you could make to your church
leadership to encourage the needed changes?

Some Areas of Equipping

In a consideration of areas where equipping is necessary, a look at certain truths is essential. These truths are based on the Ephesians 4 verses dealt with earlier in this chapter. The first truth has to do with the means by which equipping is to take place. It is the local body of Christ that must be kept in view as equipping is considered. Every Christian has a relationship with other Christians. As such, he/she is responsible for and to other Christians. The Christian church member is to be a taking as well as a giving part of the body. When a covenant relationship is established between a new member and the body, several dynamics begin to take place. One of the dynamics is that a new relationship begins that says, "I will give to you and you will give to me." The church will give training, encouragement, motivation, fellowship, and everything else necessary to equip the new family member for ministry. The new family member will give time, energy, support, and everything else to uphold the body. As the new family member grows he/she will be equipped to equip other family members.

The second truth has to do with every believer being a minister. The heart of the New Testament doctrine of the priesthood of the believer is that the believer has been saved for service. That service is his/her ministry. As a minister every believer is given a gift of a spiritual nature to use to glorify God in the building up of His church.

A third truth has to do with the equipping of believers for ministry. For a believer to function properly, there must be a penetrating study of God's Word. The Bible must be more than a book of stories and sayings. It must be the foundational truth on which the believer relies for guidance. There must be the discovery and use of spiritual gifts in Christ's service. Equipping for ministry indicates that skills must be developed for effective use.

A fourth truth has to do with the goal of equipping. The purpose of Christians being equipped is to produce growth in the body of believers. Numerical growth is only a part of the whole picture. Spiritual growth on the part of individuals is paramount. As individual believers grow in knowledge, in wisdom, and in favor with God and man, they bring growth to the whole body.

A fifth truth has to do with the "who" of equipping. The recipients of the necessary equipping for living the Christian life are the believers. The pastor has the responsibility for providing the guidance for getting the believers equipped. He has been called as a minister to

84

equip believers for ministry. His call is unique in that God has placed the responsibility of other ministers to be equipped in his hands. The pastor can know a special kind of joy as he leads in the development of others who will serve God.

The pastor sets the tone of the church. In his equipping function he has the opportunity to create an atmosphere of learning for the laity. In this atmosphere ideas and impressions can be given to enable the church to begin thinking correctly about the laypersons' roles regarding ministry.

Helping people rethink their ideas about the meaning of words related to ministry is a good beginning. Take the word "minister" itself. Traditionally we say *the* minister when referring to the pastor. The emphasis on *the* conveys the idea that only the pastor ministers. Referring to laypersons as ministers defines them as persons with a calling to service. Both pastor and laypersons are ministers.

A rethinking about the place of service would help to define the ministry of the laity. Many people think only of service at the church. In their mind's eye they see a gathered congregation and teachers/ leaders. The idea that service is performed only at church is erroneous. Service is necessary in the everyday places frequented by believers. The laity have untold opportunities to minister at work, in the home, on the streets, and other places where people are in need.

Another area the pastor influences has to do with the actual training of the laity for ministry. He is a decision-maker and as such influences others regarding their need for training. This responsibility for helping laypeople choose their training requires wisdom and insight.

If the function of the pastor is to "equip the saints for their ministry," what are some of the areas in which the laity need training? The following is given to indicate the depth and breadth of the equipping that is open to the laity and needed by them.

There are certain general areas that are needed by every Christian. All Christians need to be engaged in serious Bible study. The word *serious* is used deliberately. We not only need to study the Bible with a serious purpose, we should also be willing to give serious effort to our study. We need to understand the meaning and the message of the Bible as deeply and clearly as possible.

We need to study doctrines. The laity cannot properly minister unless they know what and why they believe as they do. Doctrine study is essential to the believer who is growing in Christ.

Knowing how the church should function as a spiritual entity and as an institution is necessary for the Christian. Knowledge of how proper organization works will benefit the believer as he or she ministers to those inside the church.

Studies of church history are necessary. We need to become familiar with the thrilling stories of those who have dared and sacrificed on our behalf in years past. We need to identify those decisions that were made and actions taken that led the church to be faithful in fulfilling God's redemptive purpose. We also need to identify those things which caused that church to be ineffective in fulfilling God's purpose.

Missions is a big area that needs to be studied. Knowledge of missions history, both foreign and home, will give the believer a familiarity with fellow believers who have sensed a call to ministry.

Studies in Christian ethics are important. The Christian believer needs to know how to make decisions concerning right and wrong. Ethical issues can confound us unless we look in depth at such problems in contemporary society as abortion, genetic engineering, and capital punishment. Christian ethics also gives us insight into handling marriage and family relationships.

These are only some of the areas in which believers need knowledge. But that knowledge is necessary if he/she is to minister to others.

A pastor will attempt to impart knowledge to those in his responsibility. He will do this using the means of the pulpit, training sessions, one-to-one studies, counselling, and various other ways to help the believers acquire knowledge.

Skill development is another big area to which the pastor as equipper must give his attention. As believers discover their spiritual gifts, the pastor can begin to provide avenues of training in developing the gifts. The gifts as listed in 1 Corinthians 12:1-11 and Ephesians 4:9-11 show a variety of skills that need to be developed. The gifts usually are not fully developed and training must be provided so that the gifted person can begin to minister effectively.

What are some of the skills that need to be developed? Here are just a few: witnessing, teaching, visiting, counselling, and administering. As you look at the spiritual gifts listed in comparison to the skills that need to be developed, it is obvious that the task of training is a big one.

Knowledge and skill development are two areas in which the pastor asserts direct influence. As knowledge is acquired and skills developed, a direct influence comes into play. The pastor's influence in an indirect way concerning the attitudes of believers is evident also.

Affirming his beliefs concerning the proper attitudes about such things as the church, calling, ministry, and others will be influential in the believer's attitude about these things.

The equipping pastor knows that the ministry of the church is to be shared by all members. By virtue of the priesthood of all believers, ministry responsibility must be assumed by the total church.

"Shared Ministry" is an emphasis of the Church Administration Department of the Sunday School Board of the Southern Baptist Convention. In the book *Shared Ministry* by Joe R. Stacker and Bruce Grubbs these principles are given as a foundation for the emphasis:

1. All believers are ministers called to serve Christ.
2. Distinctions among believers are according to function and role, not rank.
3. Ministry is the work of the whole church and the responsibility and privilege of each believer.
4. Pastoral ministry is the enabling, equipping, guiding function necessary to make the church effective in ministry.
5. Pastoral ministers should relate to each other and all believers as equals before God and in service to Christ.
6. Pastoral ministers accomplish their work best when they work as servant-leaders.
7. Prominence, authority, and influence come from faithfulness in service not position, role, or function.
8. Ministry, both that of the church and of pastoral ministers, is most effective and fulfilling when conducted according to spiritual gifts and motivated by the Holy Spirit.
9. Relationships among believers and between believers and pastoral ministers are best defined and expressed through covenants.
10. Ministry effectiveness of both the church and pastoral ministers is evaluated by both qualitative and quantitative standards.
11. Interdependency is the nature of the church's relationships both among believers and with other bodies.

The task of equipping is overwhelming. The church takes on the dimension of a miniature theological seminary for the training of ministers—the laity. The pastor becomes the chief teacher, but not the only one. He will be the teacher-equipper for the total congregation through preaching and through other activities. At times he will teach small groups in specialized areas. In the role of equipper the pastor will need the constant guidance of the Holy Spirit as he encourages, stimulates, affirms, and influences those he leads.

CHAPTER 6

HOW

LAITY

MINISTRY MAY
BE EXPRESSED

CHAPTER 6

HOW MINISTRY MAY BE EXPRESSED

The call of God to ministry is a magnificent gift and privilege God has granted to all Christians. Basically, however, the call of God to ministry is a call to responsibility. It is a call to a mission. And, although from one perspective we can rejoice in the privilege, we also are accountable before God for that ministry. In the Old Testament the Jews looked forward to what they called "the day of the Lord" (Amos 5:18, RSV). They saw this as a time of rejoicing, a time of vindication, a time of blessing. However, Amos said to them: "Woe to you who desire the day of the Lord! Why would you have the day of the Lord? It is darkness, and not light; as if a man fled from a lion, and a bear met him; or went into the house and leaned with his hand against the wall, and a serpent bit him" (Amos 5:18-19, RSV). The Jews failed to understand fully the meaning of "the day of the Lord." In a similar way it might be said that the recovery of God's call to ministry by the laity is a cause for rejoicing; it is a great recovery, but it is a recovery fraught with responsibility and accountability and should not be entered into lightly. Therefore, it is imperative that we understand with clarity what is involved in ministry and how this ministry may be expressed.

General Ministry

Everything one does may be viewed as a ministry. For example, a person may say, "I witness by the life I live." Certainly we would affirm that the life one lives is one of the most powerful witnesses a person can give, and thus this can be called a ministry. As important as this is, however, this approach seems to me to be too general even for a general ministry. "Living the Christian life" seems to me to be related more to "being a Christian" than to "being a minister."

In at least three major areas of our life we inevitably are ministers. In these areas our ministry either is based on knowledge, or it tends to be done in ignorance. It may be done haphazardly, or it may be done with conscious intent. In these areas our ministry may be effective, or it may even be negative. Thus we need to give diligent and serious study in these areas so that our expression of ministry in these areas will be both intelligent and well pleasing to God.

In family life. Much can be said and needs to be said in this area. Family relationships are so intimate that each spouse ministers to the other, and parents minister to each child. The children minister to one another and to the parents. The question is, How consciously and how intentionally Christian is this ministry? All of us feel our inadequacy in this area; yet the ministry we express is inevitable. We are grateful for the help our churches give and confess our need for still more help.

In daily life and work. Most people spend a majority of their time in the marketplace (where they work, shop, or go to school). In the marketplace choices and decisions are made that express, either positively or negatively, one's commitment to Jesus Christ as Lord of one's life.

Suppose as a Christian consumer, as a part of my ministry, I want to express a protest over the poverty and low wages paid in an emerging Third World country. Therefore, as an expression of my protest, I decide that I will refuse to purchase any article made in that country with what I see as slave-labor wages. Then someone points out to me that if everyone refused to purchase goods from that country as a protest, then the country would sell no goods, the workers would lose their jobs, and their plight would be worse than before. Then, how do I express a ministry of concern for the plight of the poor of the world?

George A. Coe, writing a number of years ago, saw the responsibility Christians have to express a ministry as a consumer. He said:

In every bargain that I make, in every article I use or consume, I traffic in human energies as well as in things. I relate myself to the health and happiness of men and women whom I have never seen. I take part in making their children what they become. To assume full responsibility for these acts of mine, to form a habit of seeing society as it is, and of tracing social causes and effects, and to think my very own moral life in community terms— these are the rudiments of an awakened, mature Christian conscience.[1]

Churches need to deal with issues similar to these so that in the practical realities as a consumer we will be better able to express our commitment to Jesus as Lord and to express our ministry in His name.

The Christian is also a worker in the marketplace. In the normal course of daily work, in meeting people, in serving people, in making decisions that affect others, in ways too numerous to mention, one has the opportunity to express ministry. Too often laypeople have not seen their life in the marketplace as a place of ministry. Therefore, if a ministry was expressed, it was only incidental or haphazard.

The church has the responsibility for developing ministers who will minister in the marketplace. The organizational structure of a church provides the means, if implemented, to recognize (discover) and train its people in meeting needs. A Sunday School class is so organized that there is an outreach ministry to those not affiliated with the church. A Church Training group has the opportunity to develop skills in ministering to the needs of those in the marketplace. Woman's Missionary Union and Brotherhood are so structured to provide ministry to the hurts of people in their daily lives.

Volumes of literature are written on the how-to's of ministering through the church. Classes using the literature are already in existence. The resources are available. What then is the problem?

The problem has to do with commitment. It requires commitment on the part of pastor, teachers/leaders, and the people needing the skill development to be involved in any type of training.

Once genuine commitment is made to discovering and developing skills related to daily work ministry, then definite plans can be made. These plans would include learning how to minister, channeling ministries to the proper places, and providing an ongoing support group for those who minister.

In the political arena. As Christians we are not only related to a family, we are not only consumers and workers in the marketplace, we are also citizens of a community, of a state, of a nation, and of a world. As such, we have both the opportunity and the responsibility to express our Christian ministry in this area as well. One way of expressing this ministry is by voting. One of the black marks against our country, our states, and our cities at this time is the low percentage of our population that exercise this right and privilege. The people who are elected and the laws that are passed affect people, and whatever affects people is an opportunity for ministry.

PERSONAL LEARNING ACTIVITY 12
What gifts do you possess for ministering to family needs? How could the church enhance those gifts?

What gifts do you have for meeting needs in the marketplace? How could the church help you exercise these gifts?

What could the church do to help you in your ministry as a citizen?

Characteristics of a Focused Ministry

I think all of us as Christians ought to seek to be Christian or give a witness or even express a ministry in our family life, in the marketplace, in the political arena, and in the whole of our lives. But I think we need to move on to what I call a "focused ministry."

If we minister only to those in our family, to those we meet in the marketplace, to those in the political arena, our ministry will be too limited. With such a limited ministry, we normally will never come in contact with many ethnic groups, many on the lower socioeconomic level whose lives are broken, whose hurts are many, whose needs are great, and who stand in need of God's ministry of reconciliation. Passing laws to help such groups is needed, surely. But these people also need a personal ministry to help them find the wholeness that only God can give. Our family, the marketplace, and politics do not normally provide us with this opportunity for personal contact and ministry with these groups of hurting people.

What, then, do I mean by a focused ministry? A focused ministry has the following characteristics. First, a focused ministry is a specific ministry. It is specific in the sense that it avoids the trap of vague generality. (An example of vague generality is "My ministry is just to love people.") It is specific in the sense that one can state what it is with clarity and can state clearly how this ministry is expressed. ("My ministry is to work with the recently divorced." "My ministry is to work with parents of exceptional children.")

Second, a focused ministry is a significant ministry. That is, it must be something that has significance and worth in terms of human need and God's redemptive purpose. It must also have significance in terms of the amount of time, energy, and effort one gives to it.

Third, a focused ministry is a ministry to which one is called by God. God not only calls the laity in general to ministry, He also calls to a specific ministry. A number of factors need to be considered in seeking to discern God's leading and God's call to a certain ministry, but an awareness of God's call is extremely important.

Fourth, a focused ministry is a ministry that is consciously self-chosen. This does not contradict what has just been said. A focused ministry is chosen because one is aware that one has been chosen and called by God to this ministry. It is not something one does because of guilty feelings. This ministry is inner motivated. It is a ministry to which one commits oneself with utmost seriousness.

Fifth, a focused ministry is a ministry for which one feels God has given him or her a gift. This personal sense of giftedness in this area should be confirmed by a small group who knows the individual intimately and also confirmed by the church as community.

94

Sixth, obviously, a focused ministry should be directly involved in fulfilling God's redemptive purpose in the world. That purpose is leading people to know Jesus as Savior and Lord in their personal lives and ministering to the human brokenness in the lives of people and society.

Areas in Which a Focused Ministry May Be Expressed

What would this ministry look like in practice? How would this kind of ministry be expressed in daily life? It seems to me that there are four major areas in which one may find his or her focused ministry? It is in response to God's call in one's life under the leadership of the Holy Spirit that a person identifies the area in which his or her focused ministry is found.

A person's focused ministry does not necessarily remain the same for the whole of his/her life. The focus of one's ministry may change from time to time.

Ministry through the structures of society. First, a person may find one's ministry through the structures of society. By structures I mean those laws, systems, mores, factors, or forces of government, education, business, and other areas of our social order that influence and tend to shape our lives. As a general rule we seek to shape the structures of society so that they are positive factors in our lives to free us to be and to do what we desire to be and to do.

How does a person express a focused ministry to the structures of society? As a general rule, to minister to or in the structures of society, one needs to be in a position of power or have access to people of power so that influence can be exerted. But this is not always the case. For example, the woman who started MADD, Mothers Against Drunk Drivers, is a typical housewife whose daughter was killed in an accident involving a drunken driver. She is having a powerful influence in changing one aspect of the structures of our society.

To give an illustration of a focused ministry to or in the structures of society, I will share the testimony of Jim. Vocationally, Jim and a partner are in business as housing consultants. His ministry is related to his vocation, but it is not done through his vocation. In 1964 Jim was appointed to be a commissioner (policy-making board member, not a full-time employee) of the Housing Authority in the city of Cambridge, Massachusetts. His church, the Old Cambridge Baptist Church, commissioned him to be God's minister of love, healing, and reconciliation at the Housing Authority. In his commissioning by his church to this ministry, Jim was told to "envelop the Authority with a sense of Christian love and concern for humankind."

The Cambridge Housing Authority is the public agency responsible for owning and managing all of the public housing in the city of Cambridge. The Cambridge Housing Authority today has a national reputation as one of the model housing authorities in the nation. Groups from major cities across the nation study their program. This does not mean that things have always gone smoothly in this ministry. But when Jim needed help, a group in his church both gave him support and also shared their ideas and insights with him. He says: "My community of faith has been a great source of energy and ideas. When we struggled with what to do at Washington Elms (a CHA housing project), I asked some OCBC [Old Cambridge Baptist church] folks to help me in my reflection. Instantly, six people volunteered to give up some of their evenings and lunches to help me work on solutions for that troubled development."[2]

Let me indicate briefly how this ministry fulfills a focused ministry. It is a specific ministry. It is a ministry to and within the Cambridge Housing Authority. I am quite sure that in the more than eight years that Jim has been involved in this ministry, he has sought to be Christian in his daily life and to be a witness in a variety of ways. The major expression of his ministry, the place of focus, the ministry to which he felt called by God and to which he was commissioned by his church was to this ministry with the Cambridge Housing authority. This was his focused ministry.

Ministry through one's vocation. A second area in which one may find one's focused ministry is through one's vocation. Certain vocations bring one naturally in contact with hurting people and with people at crisis points in their lives. Doctors, nurses, lawyers, and social workers are examples. However, whether one's vocation is school teacher, automobile mechanic, factory worker, secretary, executive, or some other vocation, one may find his or her ministry in that vocation. For example, in my first pastorate, while I was still a student in college, the chairman of the deacons was a grocer. In the most natural, in the most profound, in the most dynamic way possible, he expressed his ministry for God, day after day, in that grocery store.

Ministry through the needy areas of society. A third option a layperson may use to express one's ministry is through the needy areas of society. This option opens up an almost limitless number of opportunities. These include a ministry to the blind, the deaf, exceptional children, the poor, the alienated, the oppressed, the affluent (for they are as needy as any other group), those having marital problems, the divorced, those in prison, the unemployed, those on drugs, and on and on. Wherever in the world there are broken people and broken places, God is there working, seeking to bring the healing that only He can bring. And He is calling some of His people to join Him in these places to be instruments He can use to bring about this healing.

Illustrations of how one may express a ministry in a needy society are numerous. One such ministry has shown us what can be done through a prison ministry to help imprisoned men and women find Jesus as Lord and Savior in their lives and to help prepare them for life and society on their release from prison. A ministry through half-way homes is another ministry for prisoners.

Ministry through the organizational life of the church. The fourth and last option I will mention is a ministry through the organizational and institutional life of the churches. When I mention this, I always have to give my wife credit, because it was she who was my teacher in this area. At the time I first began to make discoveries in this area, I was disillusioned with the institutional church. At that time, nearly thirty years ago, I thought if one was going to minister for God in any serious way, that ministry had to be in a ghetto. Ministering in the ghetto was all my wife ever heard around the house. I am sure she had become "fed up" with all my ghetto talk. One day when we were talking together, with some exasperation she said to me (I'm using the terminology we used in those days): "Findley, I don't feel that God is calling me to minister to the blacks! I feel that God is calling me to minister to the Beginner children at the Crescent Hill Baptist Church!" When I reflected on what she had said, I became aware that she was more insightful than I had been. I realized afresh what I had known since childhood—that God was working in our churches and that many of the things we were doing were things that God wanted done. I realized that God was calling some of His people to teach preschool children. He called some to teach the youth and adults. But those who teach ought to do so because they have been called by God to this ministry of teaching based on the fact that they are convinced they have a gift in this area.

Those called to this ministry of teaching ought to meet weekly to minister to one another, to equip themselves for this ministry; and then they ought to make specific plans for their ministry. They ought to express their ministry (teach), meet together the next week for further equipping and planning, then do their ministry and come back together again. And what you have here is a weekly workers' meeting. But they should come together because they have been called by God to this ministry, not because the staff has put pressure on them.

Only One Major Area of Ministry

Some who read this will have three or four major leadership responsibilities at the present time in the church. They may misunderstand what I am saying, and their response will be: "Oh no! Don't add another major responsibility to my load. I'm already up to my neck in church work. I can't take on anything else!" I am not saying that you should add another major area of ministry to your already overloaded life. I am saying you should be freed from all major responsibilities except one. (There are multigifted people who will be able to be involved in more than one major area of ministry. I am not speaking of these here.) When this is said, pastors, ministers of education, and others on the church staff begin to get very apprehensive. They can just visualize wholesale resignations coming in before next Sunday.

Two things need to be said at this point. It has been estimated that 20 percent of the church members carry on the work of the church and 80 percent come along for the ride. But the doctrine of the laity says that God does not call anyone to come along for the ride. When God calls a person to become a part of His people (salvation), He also calls them to the ministry and gives them "the ministry of reconciliation." This is not some gimmick designed to get more people to work. *This is God's plan to accomplish His eternal purpose in the world*! It is time that we in the churches seriously begin trying to recover God's plan where every member is a minister instead of following a plan of our devising.

A second thing needs to be said. I know that changing the understanding, changing the attitudes, changing the conviction and commitment of the 80 percent in our churches will not be done easily, nor will it be done quickly. Therefore, to allay the apprehension of the pastors and other church staff, I recognize that having each person with only one major area of ministry is an *ideal* toward which we will work. While we are in process of moving toward the ideal, we must be practical. No one is to resign any position. However, I would recommend what one church did. One church said if any layperson felt God's call to some ministry and this ministry was affirmed by the congregation, they would free the individual from all other tasks so that he or she could fulfill God's call in his or her life.

PERSONAL LEARNING ACTIVITY 13
Does the idea of a focused ministry seem to you to be a valid approach to ministry? Why or why not? Indicate what seems to you to be points of strengths in this approach. Indicate what seems to you to be points of weakness in this approach.

Suggest other ways one might express one's ministry.

As a general rule, does the emphasis on each person's being involved in only one major area of ministry seem to you to be valid? Why or why not?

Varieties of Ministries

Paul said, "Now there are varieties of gifts, but the same Spirit; and there are varieties of service, but the same Lord; and there are varieties of working, but it is the same God who inspires them all in every one" (1 Cor. 12:4-6, RSV). One of the things these verses means is this—not everyone in the church is supposed to do the same thing. The reader may think, *That is obvious; we do not expect everyone to do the same thing in the life of the church.* Certainly that is true. Some work with children; some work with youth; some work with men and boys; some teach; some train; some administer; some work with missionary education. There are varieties of ministries in the life of the church at this time.

In the past we have tended to think that the laity could express a Christian ministry only by assuming a leadership role in the church. I do not want to be misunderstood at this point. I am not at all inferring or implying that to work in a leadership role in the organizational life of the church is not a valid, worthy, or important area of ministry. What I am saying is that this is not the *only* area of ministry for the laity. It has been estimated that a church could take care of all its major organizational leadership needs with only 20 percent of its members. This means that 80 percent of the members will find their ministry in the world. However, in the past, when we have called on the laity for a ministry, in almost every instance, it was for a ministry that was expressed in the church. It was almost as if our major concern was not to penetrate the world with the reconciling gospel. It sometimes seemed that our major concern was to keep the institution functioning. Sometimes we have been guilty of putting pressure on the laity by suggesting they prove dedication to the Lord by accepting a leadership role in the church rather than engaging in some worthy activity or ministry in the world.

God calls some to a ministry of general visitation. The ones whom God calls to this ministry ought to discern it, commit themselves to it, become equipped for it, make their specific plans, and go out and do it. And many people ought to be reached and brought into the church for worship, Bible study, and other training because these have heard God's call to the ministry of visitation and are giving themselves to it. Others are called to specific visitation (for example, discovery of gifts in fellow members).

People will be reached and brought into the church for worship, study, and training because varieties of ministry are being exercised. It may be through teaching illiterates to read. It may be through "adopting" visitors from other countries. It may be through ministering to those recently divorced. It goes on and on. You see, every person through his or her ministry is seeking to love people into the fellowship of the church where they will experience the *koinonia* of a caring Christian community and will be exposed to the preaching and study of the Word of God! One of the reasons we have placed so much emphasis on visitation is that we, as Christians, have not been "in the world," loving people and ministering to them at the points of their hurts and needs. Every Christian, through his or her ministry, is seeking to reach people for Christ. Visitation is only one—an important one—but only one means of ministry.

There are so many places of brokenness. There are so many hurting people. There are so many places of need. If it is true that I am to be involved in only one major area of ministry, and if it is true that God calls me to this special place of ministry I am to fulfill in the midst of all that needs to be done, how may I know where my place of ministry is? How may I discern God's call? It is to this we turn our attention in chapter 7.

Notes

[1]George Albert Coe, *A Social Theory of Religious Education* (New York: Charles Scribner's Sons, 1928), p. 105.
[2]*Centering,* Vol. 1, No. 1, June 1983, p. 5.

CHAPTER 7

GIFTED

LAITY

FOR MINISTRY

CHAPTER 7

GIFTED FOR MINISTRY

LAITY

God calls each of us to be a witness and a minister in all areas of our lives. In addition to this general ministry we are called to a special area for a focused ministry. In all the places where God is working, how can we discover the place of our focused ministry to which God is calling us? The answer to this question is to be found within the sphere of gifts that God has given to each Christian. One of the exciting aspects of God's call to ministry is to discover that He has gifted us to fulfill that ministry.

Spiritual gifts are mentioned four times in the New Testament— 1 Corinthians 12—14; Romans 12:3-8; Ephesians 4:11-12; and 1 Peter 4:10-11. Often pastors and laypeople alike have been hesitant to discuss or to deal with the area of spiritual gifts, because gifts were a divisive factor in the New Testament period in church history, and have been in recent times in our churches. This area abounds with questions that are exceedingly complex and difficult. Likewise quite divergent views are held by people who are equally sincere. Finally, these varying views are held with such depth and such intensity that sometimes conversation among people with differing viewpoints is quite difficult. Fortunately, it seems that this situation is changing, and people with divergent views about spiritual gifts are coming to accept one another, to trust one another, and to live and work together. This is very positive.

Our purpose in this chapter, however, is not to discuss the problems related to spiritual gifts or even to seek to give a biblical exposition of spiritual gifts. Our focus is to examine how spiritual gifts are related to God's call to ministry in our lives. Elizabeth O'Connor, in her excellent book on gifts says, "A primary purpose of the Church is to help us discover our gifts and, in the face of our fears, to hold us accountable for them."[1] When I first read that statement, I caught my breath. Did you get what she said? She said, "A primary purpose of the church is to help us discover our gifts." Perhaps she may have

104

overstated her point. However, even if we modify the statement so that it reads, "One of the major tasks of the church is to help us discover our gifts," how tragically we have missed this emphasis in the life and work of our churches. Isn't it amazing, with all the meetings, with all the emphases we have in our churches, it is only in very recent times that there has even been a mention of helping us discover our spiritual gifts? Where has this emphasis been all of my church life? It was the Church Training Department of the Sunday School Board that identified our omission and began calling it to our attention. That department provided excellent aids to help us in discovering our gift(s).

You Are Gifted

God not only has called you as a layperson to be a minister. He also has gifted you in the area He wants you to minister. You have been gifted for your ministry. Paul said, "The manifestation of the Spirit is given to every man to profit withal" (1 Cor. 12:7). Peter said, "As every man hath received the gift, even so minister the same one to another, as good stewards of the manifold grace of God" (1 Pet. 4:10). In Romans Paul's emphasis was on the fact that God's people have different gifts but this emphasis on differing gifts presupposes that all of God's people are gifted. "Having then gifts [the assumption] differing according to the grace that is given to us" (Rom. 12:6).

If you are a Christian, you are gifted. The spiritual gift was not given to you primarily for your benefit or primarily for your enjoyment. Paul said the gifts are given for profiting (1 Cor. 12:7). Peter said the gifts are given to minister to each other (1 Pet. 4:10). Gifts are for the common good and ultimately for fulfilling God's purpose in the world.

PERSONAL LEARNING ACTIVITY 14
List some of the reasons you think Christians tend to deny that they have spiritual gifts.

What do you think could be done to help Christians to accept and to affirm the fact that they have gifts?

Often I have wondered why Christians almost universally deny that they have spiritual gifts. I have come up with two possibilities. First, I think that some think to affirm that they have gifts would seem to them to be an expression of pride. For example, for a person to say, "I have the gift of teaching" or, "I have the gift of helps" could seem to the person to be bragging. And, of course, the Scripture warns us against false pride. Paul said, "I say, through the grace given unto me, to every man that is among you, not to think of himself more highly than he ought to think" (Rom. 12:3). As Christians, we want to avoid any appearance of pride. Therefore, when it is suggested that we have a gift, we protest and say, "Oh no, I don't have a gift." This makes us feel that we are being humble rather than being guilty of pride.

However, I think there is a second and more deceitful reason we deny having a gift. To whatever extent it is present, we tend not to be conscious of it. Unless I am mistaken, it is a subtle and unconscious factor with many of us. This is, if we confess that we have a gift, we become aware that we are responsible and accountable for using that gift. However, if we can convince ourselves and others that we do not have a gift, we feel justified in not accepting any responsibility. Therefore, the only way a person can avoid responsibility with a clear conscience is to insist, "I have no gift."

Gifts and Ministry Are Directly Related

If God calls the layperson to be His basic minister to a special or focused ministry and gives a gift, it is reasonable to assume that the gift and the ministry are directly related. Romans 17:6-8 makes this quite clear. Or, to put it negatively, it would seem quite strange for God to give a gift to a person and then not make use of that gift in the ministry He wants that person to fulfill. Or, it is inconceivable for

God to call a person to a certain ministry and fail to give that person the gift that would enable him or her to fulfill that ministry effectively.

Thus, one's gift(s) gives the general perimeters in which one's ministry may be found, and conversely one's ministry is a signpost pointing to the gift(s) one has. It is important, even imperative, that one identify both one's gift and one's ministry. Two approaches might be used to do this. One might first discover one's gift and then identify one's ministry within that gift. Or, one might discover one's ministry first and then identify the gift that underlies and supports that ministry. We will follow the approach of discovering one's gift first and then identifying the ministry.

An Aid in Identifying One's Gifts

Our experience in identifying our own spiritual gifts and in helping others in identifying their gifts is quite limited. The best aid with which I am familiar is produced by the Church Training Department. It is the Equipping Center module *Discovering Your Spiritual Gifts*. It can be obtained from Materials Services Department or from your Baptist Book Store. It is designed for sixteen people (two groups of eight) to spend eight sessions in study and sharing. The leader of the study may use a seminar approach or a combination of methods.

Session 1 gives an introduction to the area of spiritual gifts. In session 2 the two groups are encouraged to use the "Body of Christ" chart and indicate any gifts they perceive in themselves. In sessions 3 through 6 the two groups are led in a study of sixteen spiritual gifts. Session 7 is pivotal. On the basis of all the study and sharing they have done, each one, using the chart, indicates the gifts and the intensity of these gifts he or she sees in himself or herself. In session 8 the groups are led to consider how each one's gifts may be used in some type of church service.

In the module all of the suggested types of ministry are related to the church as an institution. Certainly ministry through the church structures is important and must not be minimized. Ministry in the marketplace also must be emphasized. A ministry for Christ must be to the church, through the church, and beyond the church.

Guidelines for Confirmation of One's Ministry

Three guidelines can be used to confirm the focused ministry that God has for you. These guidelines are not original with me. I first heard these guidelines in a conference led by Gordon Cosby, who is pastor of The Church of the Savior in Washington, DC. This is a unique church that has had a profound affect in the lives of many people and in the life of many churches since it was founded just after World War II.

The first guideline, Cosby says, is, When you find the ministry that is really for you, you will have a sense of *eureka*! *Eureka* is a Greek word that is a kind of spontaneous, joyous exclamation. For our purposes, *eureka* may be translated colloqually in a number of ways: "This is it!" "Wow! This is where it's at!" or "This is for me!" Among all of the needy places in the world and in the churches where God is working, when you find the place of your particular ministry, you will have this sense of eureka.

The second guideline is, When you find your place of focused ministry, you will dream fantastic dreams. That is, when you find your special place of ministry, you will begin to see numerous possibilities of what can be done in this area. Another way of stating this is to say you will find handles to express this ministry.

The third guideline is, When you discover your ministry, you cannot help but talk about it. You do not talk about it because someone has given you an assignment or because someone has put pressure on you; rather, you talk about it because it is so important and so meaningful to you.

Ought or overflow? When a person renders a service to someone else without knowing it or without meaning to do so, the person rendering the service unconsciously communicates the motive that underlies the service. This creates what we may call the "ought-overflow tension." That is, if a person does something for another but it is done primarily out of a sense of ought, unconsciously that sense of ought is communicated to the one receiving the service. I am aware that many things in life have to be done even if they are done out of a sense of ought. Many things in the work of the church have to be done even if they are done from a sense of ought. Not everything in life or in the church will be done from a sense of overflow.

How does one discern that ministry that one does primarily out of a motivation of overflow and also that gives one the deepest sense of eureka? (Eureka and overflow tend to go together.) One way to discern this is to ask, What is it that God is doing in the world that would give me the deepest sense of fulfillment at this time and place in my life? If you can answer that question, you may have identified the place of your ministry.

Someone may ask, Do you mean that my ministry is something I enjoy doing? This is exactly what I mean! This is where God's call and God's gift come together. This is where they mesh. Let me explain. We tend to enjoy doing any activity (or ministry) for which we are gifted. Not only that, but we also tend to be good at doing anything for which we are gifted. Conversely, we generally do not enjoy doing things for which we have no gift, and generally we do not do them well.

In terms of discovering one's ministry, what is it that leads to this sense of eureka? When God's call and God's gift intersect, when they mesh, that is what gives one the sense of eureka! God has gifted you for the ministry He wants you to do. You enjoy doing that for which you have a gift. You are good at doing the thing for which you have a gift. This means you enjoy doing the ministry the Lord has called you to do. You are good at doing the ministry that God has called you to do. Wow! This is great! No wonder we have this sense of eureka. Nor is this a shallow, superficial elation. In the deepest part of our being, we have a sense of fulfillment. We are "labourers together with God"!

Some cautions. Even God's good gifts can be misunderstood and misused. Therefore, it is necessary to point out some cautions. For example, someone may say: "Oh boy, now I don't have to do this because I don't enjoy it." Or, "Now I don't have to do that because I don't do it well." Some serious words of caution need to be given so that we do not treat this in a superficial fashion. A person may have a gift in an area and not know it. Most of us know or have heard about people who, sometimes quite by accident, discover they have a particular gift and the course of their life may be changed or the thrust of their ministry is changed. We should not rule out any area of ministry unless we have tried it, and it is confirmed that we do not have a gift. Likewise, we may have a gift in a certain area, but may not do it particularly well because we have not developed the gift. Some question whether gifts can be developed or whether they are given to the Christian fully developed.

Gifts can be developed; indeed, they must be developed. Ephesians 4:11-12 says that the ministry of the apostles, prophets, evangelists, and pastor-teachers is to equip the saints for their ministry. The saints (Christians) have been gifted by God for their ministry, but they must be equipped (developed). If one does not develop his or her gift, it is quite likely he or she may not enjoy using the gift or may not use it particularly well. In carrying out our ministry, it is imperative that we become equipped for it. In seeking to discern our gift, we must recognize that our effectiveness is partially determined by the development of our gift.

A third word of caution should be noted. Earlier it was suggested that one's ministry, based on one's giftedness, would be something that one would enjoy doing. This is true, but this does not mean that one's ministry may not be difficult. To say that one enjoys a ministry does not mean that there may not be pain, agony, and disappointment associated with it. Certainly our Lord had a deep sense of fulfillment in carrying out God's mission in the world, but He also endured deep agony in carrying it out (Heb. 12:2). But the bottom line is, God has called us to a mighty mission—His mission. He has given us a gift to enable us to fulfill that ministry. This means our ministry is something we enjoy doing, and it is something we do well. It is true, we do have to train and develop to become equipped for that ministry. But what more could God have done? Hallelujah! How can we possibly fail or refuse to respond to His call?

A fourth caution is related to the feeling of eureka. The feeling of eureka may be so strong in some that they feel their ministry is the most important in God's mission of reconciliation. They may feel everyone in the church ought to have the same sense of excitement they have about this area of ministry. They may feel that others ought to be involved in this ministry as they are. For example, those who are ministering through a certain approach to evangelism may feel that others in the church are not seriously serving God if they are not involved in the same approach to evangelism. Thus, they sometimes "lay a sense of guilt" on those who are not engaged in the particular ministry. We must take seriously Paul's emphasis that there are "varieties of gifts." "But now hath God set the members every one of them in the body, as it hath pleased him. And if they were all one member, where were the body? But now are they many members, yet but one body" (1 Cor. 12:18-20).

PERSONAL LEARNING ACTIVITY 15
Do you feel that someone else would be helpful in identifying your spiritual gifts, or do you feel you would be able to identify them best yourself?

Indicate ways you feel the three guidelines would be helpful to you in identifying your ministry.

What cautions would you add?

Often the question is asked, Does one have the same ministry for life? The answer is, Not necessarily. There are instances in which individuals do engage in the same ministry for the whole of life; for example, working with young children. But for the majority, it is possible that one's ministry may change a number of times throughout one's life. One who has the gift of teaching may express it by teaching in Sunday School for a certain period of time. Then he or she may teach high-school dropouts. At still another time the person may teach illiterates how to read. At still another time he or she may teach conversational English to nationals from other countries. Or, one may have multiple gifts and at a certain period may express a ministry utilizing a certain gift and at a different period may exercise a certain ministry using a different gift.

111

Exploring the Possibilities

How does one go about exploring what the possibilities are? The first thing that needs to be said is, Engage in ministry somewhere in some capacity while you are searching. Sometimes it may not be easy or simple for one to identify one's gift(s) or one's ministry. What may be a stumbling block is not so much identifying one's gift as it is wrestling with this matter until the individual is able to accept, to internalize, and to affirm the fact that he or she does have a gift. Sometimes our past experience and our present self-image make it difficult for us to affirm anything good about ourselves. A significant change may have to take place before some of us are able to affirm that we do have a gift. For this and other reasons, it is important that a person not take the attitude, "I don't know what my gift is, so I will not do anything until I discover my gift." God does not call any Christian to do nothing; therefore, minister somewhere while you are searching to identify your gift.

The best way I know for an individual to identify one's ministry within one's gift(s) is to try out a variety of possibilities. Generally speaking, one's gift is somewhat general in nature, and there are a number of ways one may express that gift in a ministry. For example, teaching is a gift. One may express the gift of teaching in a number of ways. One may teach children, youth, or adults in a church setting. Or one may teach illiterates to read. Or one may teach in a public school and use this vocation as the setting for ministry. Or one may teach high-school dropouts on a volunteer basis. Or one may teach conversational English to nationals from other countries. The possibilities are numerous. Thus, when one has identified one's gift(s), the problem is only half solved. The individual will need also to identify the specific ministry through which the gift is expressed. The sense of eureka will be a real help here.

After an individual has identified his or her gift, how does one go about exploring the possibilities for ministry? One of the first places one might look is in the organizational life of the church. Because we have not adequately understood the doctrine of the laity, only a limited number of church members have heard and have responded to God's call to ministry. Therefore, nearly every church has had a most difficult time finding workers. We are familiar with how every year the nominating committee in some churches has to plead to get enough people to fill the leadership responsibilities in the organizations of the church. And even then a number of willing workers are saddled with three or four jobs. This will no longer be the case when we come to understand and to practice the doctrine of the laity in our churches. But until that time comes, one of the places you may explore to see where your ministry is to be expressed is in the organizational life of the church.

However, if those who have made professions of faith and claim to be a part of the body of Christ understood and accepted God's call to ministry, the functioning needs of the institutional church could be cared for by a relatively small percentage of the typical church. This means that the large majority would find their ministry in the world. Here a person ought to explore his or her vocation to see if this is the setting in which one's focused ministry is to be found. Depending on the vocation, one often has contact with a number of people in a variety of relationships. Although most of the time the needs of these people are never verbalized, quite often they have hurts that cause deep anguish in their lives. Your ministry may be to care for someone who has a special kind of hurt. For example, one group of young adults found their ministry by dealing with the loneliness and pain of some who were recently divorced, persons with whom they came in contact through their vocation. The one whose vocation is in the home would minister to the hurts, problems, and growth needs of all in the family. But, in addition, by phone, shopping, or in visits with neighbors, this one comes in contact with broken and hurting people and may find a ministry in these settings.

Then there are the broken and hurting people whom we would not normally touch in our church life or in our vocational life. To help members become aware of the variety of areas of need, one church had social workers and workers from different agencies to come and present the problem and the need in the area in which they worked.

It is quite obvious that one would not undertake a ministry in any area without some serious study and equipping.

To conclude the options one might use in probing the possibilities for ministry (though there are many more), a need sometimes opens the door for the discovery of one's ministry. For example, a church was starting a day-care center for children. The pastor asked a woman if she would be the director of the center. Two years later the worker admitted that she had accepted the position purely from a sense of ought. She wanted to support her pastor. But this ministry became an "eureka" for her. Even though she was a college graduate, she went back to college and took a course as a part of her total equipping.

Finally, the Christian must be free to use his or her creative imagination in considering the possibilities for ministry. Having worked with laypersons for a number of years and having had them share with me the types of ministry in which they are engaged, I have been amazed at the unique and effective ways they have found to express God's ministry in the world.

Notes

[1] Elizabeth O'Connor, *Eighth Day of Creation*, copyright © 1971, p. 17; used by permission of WORD BOOKS, PUBLISHERS, Waco, Texas 76796.

PERSONAL LEARNING ACTIVITY 16

Do you know of at least one gift you have? If so, write it here.

Do you know what your ministry is within that gift? If so, write it here.

If you do not know either a gift you have or your ministry, is the possibility of discovering your gift frightening to you? Why?

Would you like to participate in a study of the Church Training Equipping Center module *Discovering Your Spiritual Gifts*? If so, check with the person responsible for special studies.

CHAPTER 8

WHERE

(PRACTICAL

DO WE GO FROM HERE?

PROPOSALS FOR IMPLEMENTATION)

CHAPTER 8

WHERE DO WE GO FROM HERE?

(PRACTICAL PROPOSALS FOR IMPLEMENTATION)

This study calls for immediate response, both by the individuals studying the book and by the corporate church. Through the text a deeper awareness should emerge of what is involved in God's call to be His people. If He calls each Christian to be a minister of His mission of reconciliation, how do we express this in life? If this, in reality, is the essence of God's call in the life of every person who claims Jesus as Lord and Savior, what should be done in the life of the corporate church to seek to make this more of a reality than it is now?

If you take these questions seriously, you will recognize immediately this will not be easy to do. As I have worked in this area with seminary students and pastor groups over the past several years, the recurring question was: "What do you do to try to make this more of a reality in the life of the church? Be specific! Be practical!" To respond to this need, this "how to" chapter has been included. Thus the last chapter is given to proposals.[1]

Background Suggestions

People will differ in their judgment as to how nearly we are achieving the ideal of the ministry of the laity or how far we are missing it. I believe our failure in expressing the doctrine of the laity is both serious and tragic. Therefore the first word of caution I would give to the pastor and people is—To make this ideal more of a reality in the life of the church will not be easy. Indeed, most have found it exceedingly difficult.

The needed change will not be brought about simply through a series of sermons. It will take time, and I am speaking in terms of years. Some whom I know have been preaching, teaching, and working in this area for several years; and the people in their churches are just now beginning to take "baby steps." Large numbers in the congregations still do not understand. So my word to you is, _Do not_ *become discouraged*.

The second thing I want to say is directed to the pastor. Certain words become so familiar to us they lose their significance for us. Normally, I would say the pastor must experience the significance of this doctrine but I am not sure that would communicate. Rather let me say I think this doctrine in the depth of its meaning must grab you at the deepest level of your life. The thing I want pastors to understand is that this is not simply a "new program" we are trying to promote. With the doctrine of the laity we are dealing with God's eternal purpose and how that purpose is to be fulfilled. We are dealing with what it means to be the church. That is central in our faith. We need not only to take it seriously; it must become very personal for us. Robert Greenleaf, who for a number of years was Director of Management Research for AT&T, says: "Not much happens without a dream. And for something great to happen, there must be a great dream. Behind every great achievement is a dreamer of great dreams. Much more than a dreamer is required to bring it to reality; but the dream must be there first."[2] My second word then is, *Have a dream*.

A pastor should have some conferences with the other members of the church staff and their spouses. The Scripture says, "Can two walk together, except they be agreed?" (Amos 3:3). I think it is imperative that the total staff of the church have the same philosophy (theology) concerning the life and work of the church, seeking harmoniously to lead the church in the same direction. Experiential disharmony in philosophy can be painful for the staff members and result in confusion for the church. My third word then is, *Seek harmony*.

Remember, we are dealing with background factors that will affect what the pastor and people undertake to do. Another factor the pastor needs to note is that of leadership style. This is a tremendously important as well as complex area. It is also an area where there are strong differences of opinion.

Limited research has been done regarding leadership style and the ministry of the laity. The initial findings suggest that a style which expresses openness, vulnerability, and a sharing of leadership enhances the emergence of the ministry of the laity. Again Greenleaf has a word for us. Says he, "Perhaps, as with the minister and the doctor, the servant-leader might also acknowledge that his own healing is his motivation. There is something subtle communicated to the one who is being served and led if, implicit in the compact between the servant-leader and led, is the understanding that the search for wholeness is something they share."[3] This applies not only to the pastor in his relations with church members; it applies also to the laity as they relate to those to whom they minister. My fourth word then is, _Consider your leadership style_.

Some Difficulties to Be Faced

A major problem, and perhaps the fundamental one, is the inherent difficulty involved in trying to become a people who are called to be ministers. Although there are those in our churches who understand what this means and who are expressing their ministry, many do not understand. They may become frightened at the prospect of having to minister. They may have the philosophy that "religion" is a good thing if having all of God's blessings requires only believing in Jesus, attending church fairly regularly, and living a good moral life. But this idea of being a minister is something else.

There may be hesitancy to lead the church to pursue and practice the doctrine of the laity because we do not want to go against those who do not agree with it. But, difficult as it is, the group will either make a decision to do something or make a decision not to do something. And they make that decision under God.

Some practical questions the group needs to face are as follows: How can the larger congregation become aware of what is involved in the doctrine of the priesthood of all believers? What can we do to go beyond the level of awareness and begin to develop a serious understanding of what it means to be the people of God? But understanding, as essential as it is, does not always lead to action. What can we do to help the people to become motivated to the point where they are willing to be ministers of God's mission of reconciliation in the world? How do we develop conviction? How do we help people to develop their inner life so they will have the spiritual foundation to invade the world of brokenness with God? How do we help people to understand in a practical and specific manner how ministry is expressed in God's world? How do we help people discover and "own" their spiritual gift(s)? How can we help people identify their focused ministry? What should the church do to help equip people for their ministry? How can the church provide support for God's ministers in the world? How can we maintain unity in the midst of diversity? How can we minister meaningfully to those in the congregation who either do not understand or do not agree with this perspective? If any conflict comes, how can we make it creative?

120

Developing Awareness

The concern of this section is with the level of awareness. Most Baptists are aware that there is a doctrine we hold dear called the priesthood of all believers. We would also like for them to be aware that growing out of this doctrine is the concept of the ministry of the laity. We would like for them to be aware that while we have done many good things as Christians, our ministry as laypersons has been tragically weak.

The practical suggestions given in the remaining part of the chapter, though divided into sections, are really all of one piece. The divisions are more academic than real. Few of the suggestions given can be limited to one section.

Recognizing that a majority of the congregation will not have studied this book, what can be done to help them become aware of the doctrine of the laity and the hope and promise it offers for the fulfilling of God's redemptive purpose in the world? Obviously the best way to get an exposure to the largest number of people would be for the pastor to preach a series of sermons in this area in the Sunday morning worship service. Added to this, as a way of beginning to deepen their understanding in this area, would be for the pastor to have talk-back sessions on Sunday night. A broad outline of the sermon could be given on a half sheet of paper which would be given out on Sunday morning. The people would be encouraged to write any comment or question that comes to them while listening to the sermon. The questions may ask for clarification or for additional information. Or the question may deal with a point where there seems to be a disagreement. It should be pointed out that disagreements are not bad. A talk-back session gives the pastor the opportunity to elaborate on points where time was not available on Sunday morning.

Another possibility is to have a series of Bible studies related to the doctrine of the laity during the Wednesday evening prayer service. For most churches the size of the group on Wednesday evening would permit dialogue which would enhance the study.

Whatever choices are made about presenting this doctrine to the total congregation or to groupings within the congregation, be sure that the presentations are biblically based. Southern Baptists are a biblically oriented people. If they can be shown that the doctrine of the laity comes from the Bible, they will tend to accept it.

Another resource for helping develop awareness is *The Priesthood of the Believer,* an Equipping Center module from the Church Training Department. This is an excellent eight-session study and is highly

121

recommended. The Brotherhood Commission has a six-session study entitled, *Bold New Laity*. This gives a brief introduction to the history of this doctrine.

Using the resources listed below and others the group will suggest, build up the church media library in this area.

RESOURCES

Costa, Orlando E., *The Church and Its Mission*
Diehl, William E., *Christianity and Real Life*
Diehl, William E., *Thank God, It's Monday!*
Edge, Findley B., *The Greening of the Church*
Edgemon, Roy, Compiler, *Developing Believers—a Church Training Manual*
Holms, Urban T., III, *Spirituality for Ministry*
Mouw, Richard J., *Called to Holy Worldliness*
Newby, James R., *The Creation of a Future*
Stacker, Joe and Grubbs, Bruce, *Shared Ministry*
Snyder, Howard A., *Liberating the Church: the Ecology of Church and Kingdom*
Wallis, Jim, *The Call to Conversion: Recovering the Gospel for These Times*

Newsletters
Centering
The Center for Ministry of the Laity
210 Herrick Road
Newton Centre, MA 02159
Laos in Ministry
Lutheran Church in America
231 Madison Avenue
New York, NY 10016

The people in your church should be encouraged to read one or more of the many good books in this area. Reading this would develop their awareness and deepen their understanding. There are several ways one may do this. In the period of announcements before the worship service begins, the pastor may tell briefly about one or two books he has found meaningful and indicate these may be secured from the church media library. One church had a book table on Wednesday night as the people came for the family night dinner. The books were displayed on a table as the people passed by in line. A person was there to assist those who wanted to get a book.

Recognizing the hesitancy of some people to read books, the pastor can take a carefully selected book to a particular individual. Because of the knowledge the pastor has of the members, he would know of some who would be quite responsive to the emphasis on the doctrine of the laity.

Another suggestion for developing awareness is to appoint an existing group such as the church council to serve as a committee to work with the pastor. This group would assess where the church is with reference to the doctrine of the laity. They would discuss alternatives of what may be done next to help the church move forward in the area of understanding, accepting, and fulfilling the ministry of the laity. The pastor needs a group of laypersons who can give their evaluation as to how the members of the congregation are hearing and reacting to what is being done in the area of the ministry of the laity. They can also serve as a sounding board as options of what may be done next are considered. The pastor also needs for them to serve as a personal support group.

Deepening Understanding

Awareness is simply helping people become conscious that something exists. In seeking to deepen understanding, we are undertaking to give them a clearer comprehension of the doctrine of the laity—its biblical base, its importance, how it is expressed, how God has enabled us for this ministry. Therefore when they think about this issue and consider the possibility of making a decision about it, they can do so with intelligence.

The approach to deepening understanding generally will need to be done in smaller groupings where there is the opportunity for dialogue. Retreats offer an excellent setting for this to take place. The retreat also gives the individual an opportunity, momentarily, to get away from the telephone, from the responsibilities, and from the busyness of life. This gives the individual the opportunity to focus in a deeper and more concentrated manner upon the matter being considered.

There are three groups I would suggest ought to be planned for as early as possible: First, the church staff and spouses; second, the deacons and spouses; and third, Sunday School and Church Training leadership.

Another thing that might be done to deepen understanding is to invite a pastor or a solid layperson to visit the church to share what is happening in his/her life and church.

Magnify the church media library. Again, my experience has been when people catch the dream in this area they begin to read. The church media library ought to become a beehive of activity as people seek information about the Bible, about the equipping needed, and about issues we face in our world.

Also try to find a way to change the language of the people concerning *minister, the ministry, call to the ministry, clergy,* and the like. Obviously, the pastor and other staff should set the example. Discuss with the deacons and others what they feel is the best way to do this.

Finally, modeling is crucial. One of the problems we face in our churches is the conflict between what we say and what we do. In the worship services, Sunday School, Church Training, and in the missionary organizations, we hear and speak all the high ideals and demands of the Christian faith. But often there is not serious expression of them in our lives. We know we ought to be a loving, caring, redemptive people, but in the main we really do not know how this would be expressed. What we need in our churches to give a deeper understanding of the ministry of the laity are models who are expressing ministry in their lives. We need more than words; we need a model. In every church at least a few either express a ministry or are ready to do so. Identify these people. Free them from other responsibilities if necessary. Equip them. Encourage them to look at ministry avenues through WMU and Brotherhood mission action groups. Commission them. And in the spirit of a servant, let them fulfill their ministry. We need individuals and churches who serve as models.

PERSONAL LEARNING ACTIVITY 17
In terms of your personal feelings and attitude, how important is it for the church to understand and express the doctrine of the laity? Please express your answer by placing an X on the scale below.

Frankly, it   **I feel**
does not seem 0 _____100   **it is**
   important   10 20 30 40 50 60 70 80 90 100 **imperative.**
   to me.

Please list the reasons for your answer.

If you feel the church ought to do more than is now being done to express the doctrine of the laity, what is the first thing that ought to be done to help the church develop awareness?

What do you think ought to be done to help the members of the church deepen their understanding of this doctrine?

Developing Conviction

Understanding the doctrine of the laity and the call of God in our lives, important as this is, does not necessarily lead to action. We also face the problem of seeking to lead people to understand and believe this doctrine with such depth they become willing to do something about it. What can we do to work with the Holy Spirit that He may bring conviction in the lives of people in this area?

For most of us, one essential factor in this process is a deeper personal relationship with God. When we begin to consider seriously the possibility of invading the world with God to seek the healing and redemption of broken people, many of us are brought to face the shallowness of our own relationship with God. Those of us who have met God at one level of our lives are made aware that we need to meet Him at a much deeper level in our lives.

Many churches have found that The Church Renewal Journey, sponsored jointly by the Evangelism Department of the Home Mission Board and the Brotherhood Commission, has been a significant aid in helping many laypeople to meet God at a deeper level in their lives. The interaction of laypeople with laypeople is quite significant in this experience. When a church member sees another layperson— a plumber, a doctor, a housewife, a truck driver, a policeman, an executive—whose life has been transformed, even after his or her conversion experience; this causes the church member to think deeply about his or her own life.

One minister of education has developed this deepening of conviction by focusing on the leadership of the organizations of the church. Through individual conferences with the leadership, retreats, tapes, books and articles, over a period of a year or more, the leadership began to catch a new vision of the work of the various organizations. They studied why organizations lose their zeal and what needs to be done to recover that zeal. Using as resources such books as: *Redreaming the Dream* by Robert Dale; *A Church On Mission* by Reginald McDonough; and *The Church: Change or Decay* by Michael Tucker, the leadership developed a deeper motivation for the work they were doing. He says: "Our leaders decided no longer would it be just church work, but we needed to begin the work of the church! No longer would we do 'business as usual.' Rather we would get down to business! Ministry began to happen."

Also as an essential part of developing conviction and meeting God at a deeper level is a continuing emphasis on deepening the inner life. Numerous books have been written which the pastor will find helpful in leading the people in this area. Let me list a few devotional aids people might find useful.

Classics of Christian Devotion

Augustine, Saint, *Confessions*
Brother Lawrence, *The Practice of the Presence of God*
Bunyan, John, *The Pilgrim's Progress*
Law, William, *A Serious Call to a Devout and Holy Life*
Pascal, Blaise, *Pensees*
Woolman, John, *The Journal of John Woolman*

Books by People of Devotion
   Bonhoeffer, Dietrich, *Letters and Papers from Prison*
   Delp, Alfred, *Prison Meditations*
   Kelly, Thomas R., *A Testament of Devotion*
   Merton, Thomas, *The Seven Storey Mountain*
   Steere, Douglas, *On Beginning from Within*
Meditations
   Baillie, John, *A Diary of Private Prayer*
   Chambers, Oswald, *My Utmost for His Highest*
   Hammarskjold, Dag, *Markings*

In addition to this emphasis on the personal life of Christian devotion, I strongly recommend the use of *MasterLife* for every church. Write to the Church Training Department of the Sunday School Board in Nashville for additional information. This is a serious, experiential approach that focuses on the spiritual life. The Evangelism Department of the Home Mission Board has an eight-hour seminar, "Prayer for Spiritual Awakening," which is provided for local churches. They also sponsor regional and Convention-wide seminars in this area.

The importance of deepening conviction cannot be overemphasized. At the present time there are many things regarding God's work we know we ought to do; we simply do not have the depth of conviction to lead us to do it.

PERSONAL LEARNING ACTIVITY 18
As you know, conviction (for people to be willing) is fundamental to this whole doctrine of the laity. What percent of the members of your church do you think have the depth of conviction to be willing, in a serious way, to give practical expression to this doctrine? Write your answer below.   *30%*

If your estimate tends to be low, give the reason or reasons you think there is not a larger percent.
   NOT SURE

Using the suggestions given here and your own ideas, list the two most important things that ought to be done in your church to try to deepen commitment on the part of all members.

VISITING AS AN EXPRESSION OF INTREST IN THE PEOPLE

Becoming Involved in Ministry

A number of proposals for practical implementation have been made in the various chapters of the book. These ought to be reviewed. With regard to helping the members of the church discover or identify their gifts, I suggest you start with the Church Training Equipping Center module, *Discovering Your Spiritual Gifts*.

Another approach to helping a person understand the concept of a *call* from God is to lead the people in a study of the variety of *calls* that came to different people in the Bible. Along with this, one could study the life and ministry of these individuals and identify gifts which they seem to have for their ministry.

The equipping of church members will depend on where they are along the continuum from awareness of God's call to involvement in ministry. Some members will need help in one area, others will need help in another. This makes the equipping task all the more difficult. However, we must be aware that the various church organizations are giving general, and sometimes specific, equipping in a variety of areas. Thus we should seek to identify the specific areas of equipping in which the members need help most.

One area which we have emphasized time and again in our

churches but which still needs special emphasis is in the matter of personal witnessing. The Evangelism Department of the Home Mission Board has some excellent training available in this area. "TELL Witness Training" may be used by an individual or in a group setting. It uses a LaBelle Duo 16 projector and specially prepared cartridges. There are twelve one-hour sessions. "Lay Evangelism School" is for adults and youth. It involves careful planning, an intensive week of training, and three months of on-the-job training. "Continuing Witness Training" involves thirteen weeks of intensive Bible study, the development of practical skills, and the memorization of a model presentation.

The Equipping Center module, *How to Witness,* is a six-session study. The module can be studied in a small group setting or by a one-to-one approach. Ten sessions are suggested if the one-to-one approach is used. *How to Witness* offers practical, on-the-job training to Christians in how to witness with their lips as well as their lives. It will help them to apply the principles of "life-style witnessing." Another module, *Training Sunday School Workers in Evangelism,* can be used to train Sunday School workers to witness.

In addition to the various modules in the Equipping Center which are designed to equip the laity, the Church Training Department has developed LIFE (Lay Institute for Equipping). LIFE will provide advanced level training in quarter-long courses. The participants will engage in individual study and on-the-job training. In addition, there will be a weekly one to two hour seminar in which the participant is led to reflect upon and evaluate his/her study and experience. Leaders for these courses will be trained in special workshops using BTN (Baptist Telecommunication Network) programs and through special leader guides.

Another special study for the laity is *MasterDesign: Your Calling as a Christian.* The purpose of this study is to provide a biblical foundation for the ministry of the laity; to provide in-depth study material for MasterLife alumni and others; and to serve as a foundation for lay leadership training. This study enables learners to express, explain, and defend their beliefs about the calling of all Christians to become ministers. The Book of Ephesians is used to explore the responsibility of all Christians to discover their gifts, to develop them, to be trained by God-given equippers, and to minister to the church and the world.

Some in the church already know both their gift and their ministry. Many of them are already doing their ministry. They need to become

130

a part of a WMU or Brotherhood mission action group, become equipped, and then be commissioned by the church. Certainly over the years they have become equipped, at least to some degree, for their ministry. If they feel they need additional training, the pastor-equipper will help them find resources.

Most of the ministry in which we Christians have been engaged has been a ministry related to the organizational life of our churches. This area of ministry is both necessary and significant. We need to have more ministry in this area, and we need to do it even better. Our ministry in the marketplace and in other parts of society has been relatively limited. The more experience we have in this area, the more resources we will have to equip them; and the more experiences we will have upon which to base suggestions for helping them.

In conclusion, what can a pastor expect with reference to helping this doctrine to be expressed in the life of the members of the congregation? As stated earlier, it does not happen quickly. Our conditioning is to look for programs that bring immediate success. If success is not forthcoming, we abandon it and move on to something else. This expectation and approach will have to be changed rather drastically. A pastor must look at the implementation of this doctrine as a long range and continuing emphasis. It certainly cannot be done in a short pastorate.

The doctrine of the laity is biblical. It is God's plan for fulfilling His redemptive mission in the world. Regardless of the response of the people, regardless of the time it will take, regardless of the cost to each of us, we have no choice but to seek to make it real in our own lives and in the life of the church. The church is the "body of Christ." We who are the church must be where Christ would be in the world doing what He would be doing if He were here in the flesh. This is what the doctrine of the laity is all about!

Notes

[1] I was unwilling to trust my limited experience to make these proposals alone. Therefore, I asked for suggestions from the following (obviously I am responsible for what is written here): Lewis Abbott, pastor, Lexington Baptist Church, Lexington, SC; Richard Broholm, Director, The Center for the Ministry of the Laity, Andover Newton Theological School, Newton, MA; William Clemmons, Professor of Christian Education, Southeastern Baptist Theological Seminary, Wake Forest, NC; Eddie Hammett, minister of education, Leawood Baptist Church, Greenville, SC; Ken Smith, pastor, Fellowship Baptist Church, Tallahassee, FL.
[2] Robert K. Greenleaf, *Servant Leadership*. (New York: Paulist Press, 1977), p. 16. Used by permission.
[3] Ibid. p. 36.

Teaching Guide

by
Mic Morrow

Introduction

This teaching guide gives detailed planning for five sessions. Careful planning will allow you to cover the material for either large or small groups. Visual aid ideas and worksheet masters have been included for the enhancement of the study.

Preplanning

Do the following things well in advance of the sessions:

1. Order adequate copies of *The Doctrine of the Laity*. Distribute these at least a week prior to the first session as an enlistment technique.
2. Publicize the study using announcements in worship services and church organizational meetings, making posters giving the schedule of the sessions, writing cards and letters to potential participants, and personally inviting selected people who especially need this emphasis on the laity.
3. Read the entire text making notes as you do. Complete the personal learning activities. Read the teaching guide and mark those activities that will require duplicating worksheets, making visual aids, and/or compiling teaching materials.
4. Read the Church Study Course information in the back of the book. Plan how you will keep records of enrollment, participation, and application for Church Study Course credit.

Session Planning

Five sessions are suggested for teaching this book. Consideration should be given to the amount of time for each session and how much material you want to cover. The teaching plans are guides and should be used depending on each local situation.

Here are some suggestions for teaching each session:

1. Arrange the meeting room so that participants will sense a good learning atmosphere.
2. Have the worksheets, visual aids, and teaching materials ready before the session.
3. Have extra copies of the text and the Bible.
4. Arrive early so you can greet each participant. For early arrivers, plan some simple activities to be done before the session begins.
5. Begin on time and end on time.
6. Be flexible. Remember that the teaching plan is just a guide. Try to meet the needs of the participants by answering questions as they arise.
7. Express feelings of enthusiasm about what you are teaching.
8. Pray before, during, and after each session for God's guidance.

Session 1
Introduction, Chapters 1 and 2

Session goal: After completing this session, participants should have a better understanding of God's people as unique. Participants will be able to: (1) explain the essence of the uniqueness of Christians; (2) compare Israel and new Israel; (3) summarize what the conversion experience is; (4) explain how the foundation for the motivation for ministry is found in the conversion experience; and (5) tell one specific action to give evidence of being a part of God's people.

Before the Session

1. Have copies of *The Doctrine of the Laity* on hand for those who do not have a copy. Ask someone to be responsible for registering participants. Get a Baptist Doctrine Diploma.
2. Make an overview poster giving the session goals (visual aid 1).
3. Have a chalkboard and chalk available.
4. Get a dictionary definition of *unique*.
5. Make four placards: Abraham, Isaac, Jacob, and Moses (visual aid 2).
6. Prepare a lecture on "God Calls a People" using these key words as guides: *gift, condition, priests, failed,* and *mission.*
7. Duplicate worksheet 1.
8. Prepare an outline poster of chapter 2 (visual aid 3). Display it. Put strips of adding machine tape across the points you will cover.

During the Session

1. Welcome each participant as he/she arrives. Register each one. Give each one a copy of *The Doctrine of the Laity* if he/she does not have the book. Make this assignment: Read the Introduction and be ready to tell the purpose of each chapter and the meaning of *laity.*
2. Begin the session with a get-acquainted activity. Ask each person to introduce himself/herself by giving name and number of years as a Christian. Add the number of years up and comment on what that amount of years should mean regarding the upbuilding of the church.
3. Explain the requirements of study course credit. You will find an explanation of the requirements at the end of the book. Show the Baptist Doctrine Diploma and encourage each person to earn one.
4. To give an overview of the entire study call on several participants to tell the purpose of each chapter. Display the overview poster. Give the teaching schedule. Read each session goal. Call on a participant to give the meaning of *laity.*
5. Read aloud the session goal for session 1. Ask, What are synonyms (words or phrases meaning the same thing) for *the people of God*? As answers are given write them on the chalkboard. Clarify any words or phrases that may not be understood.

6. Read a dictionary definition of *unique*. Ask volunteers to tell how Christians are unique. Lead a discussion of the question in personal learning activity 1.

7. Comment on the author's statements: "I was forced to conclude that while a Christian certainly ought to strive to live as good and as moral a life as possible, this is not what makes the Christian unique" and "I was certain that God was interested in something deeper than how I related to the church as an institution."

8. Display across the top of the chalkboard the placards with the names of Abraham, Isaac, Jacob, and Moses on them. Give a brief lecture on "God Works Through Individuals," telling how God worked through the four men to bring humankind back to Himself. As you talk about each person, draw an arrow from one to the other. From the Moses placard draw an arrow to the middle of the chalkboard. Write in big bold letters the word *PEOPLE*.

9. Read aloud Exodus 19:5-8. Lecture on "God Calls a People." Ask participants to underline key words in this section as you lecture. Use the following key words as the thrust of your lecture: *gift, condition, priests, failed,* and *mission.*

10. Call on volunteers to answer the two questions in personal learning activity 2. Discuss the answers.

11. Explain what the author means in the section "Jesus Confronts the Scribes and Pharisees" when he says "They thought God had called them to be a *separated people* rather than a *people on mission.*"

12. Distribute worksheet 1. Ask each participant to read "The New Israel" and answer the questions on the worksheet. Call attention to the assignment on the worksheet. Ask group members to complete this as an after-class assignment.

13. Refer to the outline poster of chapter 2. Lecture on the entire chapter. As you talk about the different points, pull away the adding machine tape from those points.

14. Put the participants in groups of three. Assign one of the three to be a listener. The other two are to review what has been said in this session and discuss the relationship between conversion and motivation. The listener should jot down notes for reporting to the large group. Call the group together. Ask several listeners to report what they heard.

15. Close with a prayer that we as Christians might see ourselves as the unique people of God with the purpose of fulfilling God's mission in the world.

134

Session 2
Chapters 3 and 4

Session goal: After completing this session, participants should have a better understanding of the ministry of the laity and the nature of God's mission/our mission. Participants will be able to (1) define the meaning of the priesthood of all believers; (2) explain the call to ministry of the laity; (3) identify the nature of God's mission; and (4) state a way to be involved personally in God's mission.

Before the Session

1. Enlist a member to tell briefly what was done in the last session.
2. Display the overview poster.
3. Make statement strips from "The Meaning of the Priesthood of All Believers" (visual aid 4).
4. Prepare a lecture on "What Does the Bible Say?"
5. Get Bibles for those who need them.
6. Duplicate worksheet 2.
7. Make the outline poster on "Social Involvement" (visual aid 5).
8. Write this question on the chalkboard: Can the churches emphasize both evangelism and social involvement and not neglect either? Cover the question with paper.
9. Enlist someone to represent evangelists from 1830 to 1865.
10. Duplicate worksheet 3.

During the Session

1. Greet members warmly. Introduce new participants. Call on the enlisted person to tell briefly what was done in the last session. Lead in a prayer asking God to make us receptive to truths about the ministry of the laity in God's mission.
2. Refer to the overview poster to show the focus of this session.
3. Ask volunteers to tell their interpretation of the term the *priesthood of the believer*. Using the introductory material in chapter 3, contrast the Roman Catholic and Southern Baptist views of the priesthood of all believers.
4. Display the statement strips giving the main thoughts of the section "The Meaning of the Priesthood of All Believers." Explain each one.
5. Divide the group into three small groups. Ask each small group to discuss one each of the questions in personal learning activity 5. After ample time call the group together. Ask a representative from each small group to report on the discussions.
6. Lecture on "What Does the Bible Say?" Ask the participants to read aloud the Bible verses you will explain.
7. Pair up group members. One is to be a reader. This person will read aloud to his/her partner the section "An Incarnational Ministry" from the beginning through the paragraph following the situation of Mrs. Smith. The

partner is to jot down words or phrases as notes. The partner has the responsibility of explaining what incarnational ministry means after the reading.

8. Distribute worksheet 2 and Bibles. Write the term *Personal Salvation* on the chalkboard. Comment that knowing what sin is and knowing the remedy for sin is essential in personal salvation. Ask participants to complete the worksheet. Call on volunteers to share their answers.

9. Read aloud the two questions in personal learning activity 8. Ask for responses.

10. Display the outline poster on "Social Involvement." Lecture on the section "Social Involvement" following the outline.

11. Ask participants to answer the three questions in personal learning activity 9. After ample time discuss the second question.

12. Uncover the question on the chalkboard: Can the churches emphasize both evangelism and social involvement and not neglect either? Call on the person who has been enlisted to represent evangelists from 1830 to 1865 period. Ask him these questions: (1) What evidence is there that evangelical religion supports social concerns? (The answer is Edward Beecher's statement.) (2) What group is a good example of one that had a fervent evangelistic witness and a concern for persons in their social needs? (Answer: The Salvation Army.) (3) What did Henry Ward Beecher say about changing laws and structures of society that permitted human exploitation? (Answer: Read statement from book.) (4) Name some famous evangelists of the past who were opposed to the social disgrace, slavery. (Answer: Joshua Leavitt, George B. Cheever, and John Wesley.) (5) Since John Wesley is the most famous of these evangelists, what evidence do we have that he balanced the emphases of personal salvation and social involvement? (Answer: Read the preface of his 1739 Hymn Book and the statement by Bready.)

13. Distribute worksheet 3. Ask members to complete it as an after-class assignment.

14. Close with a prayer of commitment that as Christians we will fulfill our ministry through evangelical and social avenues.

Session 3
Chapter 5

Session goal: After completing this session, participants should have a better understanding of the role of the pastor as equipper. Participants will be able to: (1) identify biblical material related to calling; (2) define the task of the pastor; and (3) describe some areas where equipping is necessary.

Before the Session

1. Display the overview poster.
2. Prepare a lecture on the section "A Brief Biblical View."
3. Get paper and pencils for each person.
4. Prepare a lecture on "Some Areas of Equipping."
5. Make a poster on truths based on Ephesians 4 (visual aid 6).
6. Make phrase strips on areas in which laity needs training (visual aid 7).

During the Session

1. Welcome each arriving participant. Introduce any new members to the group. Remind conferees that this course is for at least five hours. Church Study Course credit will be granted to those who attend all sessions and read the book.
2. Call on volunteers to tell one thing learned during the last session.
3. Refer to the overview poster. Read the session goal for session 3.
4. Lecture on the section "A Brief Biblical View." Encourage participants to use their Bibles to read the selected verses on which you lecture.
5. Give each person a pencil and sheet of paper. Ask each one to write down his/her understanding of the task of the pastor. When this is done, divide participants into four small groups. Assign each small group one each of the sections under "The Task of the Pastor." They are to read the material preceding the first section and their assigned section. After ample time they are to discuss their section and write down key ideas. Call the group back together and ask representatives to report on the discussions.
6. Lead in a group discussion of the questions in personal learning activity 11.
7. Display the poster of truths based on Ephesians 4. Point out each truth as you explain what it means. Use the material in "Some Areas of Equipping." Lecture on areas in which the laity needs training. As you speak display the phrase strips on these knowledge and skill areas.
8. Announce the subjects of the next session—the expression of ministry and spiritual gifts. Encourage each person to be present. Ask members to invite fellow Christians who have not attended the other sessions to be present.
9. Close with a prayer that each participant would be supportive of the pastor as equipper by following his guidance in finding his/her place of ministry.

Session 4
Chapters 6 and 7

Session goal: After completing this session, participants should have a better understanding of ways ministry may be expressed and giftedness. Participants will be able to: (1) describe how ministry may be expressed; (2) identify an aid for discovering spiritual gifts; and (3) identify ways to express spiritual gifts in ministry.

Before the Session

1. Display the overview poster.
2. Make a poster of statements which may be true or false from chapter 6 (visual aid 8). Make small *yes* and *no* signs for each member. (Suggestion: The *yes* signs could be pieces of green paper and the *no* signs could be pieces of red paper.)
3. Prepare a poster listing the spiritual gifts (visual aid 9).
4. Prepare a lecture on the section "You Are Gifted" from chapter 7.
5. Secure the Equipping Center module *Discovering Your Spiritual Gifts*.
6. Duplicate worksheet 4.
7. Enlist a person who has discovered his/her gift and ministry to tell about the discovery and how he/she ministers. This person should refer to "Exploring the Possibilities."

During the Session

1. Welcome participants. Ask three volunteers to tell at least one significant thing learned in the previous three sessions.
2. Call attention to the overview poster. Read the session goal for this session. Write the words *expression of ministry* and *spiritual gifts* side by side on the chalkboard. Ask the group to call out words or phrases that define or clarify these terms. Write these under the two terms. Comment that the session will deal with how the laity may express ministry and how spiritual gifts may be used in that ministry.
3. Display the poster of the true or false statements from chapter 6. Give each person a *yes* sign and a *no* sign. Read each statement aloud. As each statement is read, ask for agreement (holding up the *yes* sign) or disagreement (holding up the *no* sign). If everyone agrees with the statement, make some additional comments for clarification. Then move on. If there are those who disagree with the statement, ask why. Give those who disagree a chance to explain their reasons for disagreeing. Give other group members an opportunity to comment. Use the information in the chapter to clear up any confusion, misunderstandings, or misguided thoughts.

(During the report and discussion on focused ministry and having only one major area of ministry, ask participants to do personal learning activity 13.)

4. Display the poster listing the spiritual gifts from 1 Corinthians 12—14;

138

Romans 12:3-8; Ephesians 4:11-12; and 1 Peter 4:10-11. Inform the group that the purpose of this section is not to do a study of the spiritual gifts, but to examine how spiritual gifts are related to God's call to ministry.

5. Read aloud the statement made by Elizabeth O'Connor and the sentences that follow in that section.

6. Lecture on the section "You Are Gifted" in chapter 7. Ask participants to do personal learning activity 14.

7. Show the Equipping Center module *Discovering Your Spiritual Gifts*. Using the information in the section "An Aid in Identifying One's Gifts" give an overview of the module.

8. Distribute worksheet 4. Tell members to read the section "Guidelines for Confirmation of One's Ministry" and fill in the blanks on the worksheet. After this is done, go over the statements and clarify any points needing further explanation.

9. Call on the enlisted person to tell how he/she explored the possibilities of ministry and how he/she discovered what his/her gift(s) and ministry were. Encourage this person to use the section, "Exploring the Possibilities."

10. Divide the group into three small groups. Appoint a leader for each small group. Tell each group to discuss each question in personal learning activity 16. Call for a summation from each leader.

11. Explain that the last session will be a learning/planning session. Ask group members to come prepared to make some plans concerning (1) what they will do in the area of ministry and (2) what they will propose the church should do to implement what has been learned.

12. Close with a prayer for guidance that each person will make right decisions for becoming involved in ministry.

Session 5
Chapter 8

Session goal: After completing this session, participants should have a better understanding of how the doctrine of the laity can be implemented. Participants will be able to: (1) identify an awareness, an understanding, and a conviction about involvement in ministry; and (2) make plans for personal and church implementation of laity involvement.

Before the Session

1. Prepare a lecture on "Background Suggestions."
2. Make four signs giving the heart of the message (visual aid 10).
3. Get three large sheets of poster paper, masking tape, and three felt-tip markers.
4. Get the Equipping Center module *The Priesthood of the Believer* and any books suggested in chapter 8.
5. Enlist several persons to comment briefly on two or three books from the list under "Developing Conviction."
6. Duplicate worksheet 5.

During the Study

1. Welcome participants to this session. Take care of any business related to Church Study Course credit.
2. Review the previous sessions by reading the session goals on the overview poster.
3. Comment on the uniqueness of the last chapter in *The Doctrine of the Laity*. Tell the group that during this last session decisions will be made for implementing what has been learned in the previous sessions.
4. Lecture on the section "Background Suggestions." As you lecture, display the signs giving the heart of your message.
5. Tell group members to read silently the section "Some Difficulties to Be Faced." Ask each person to underline what he/she considers to be the one or two most important questions. After ample time, call on several to tell which questions they underlined. Allow other participants to provide some answers. Comment that this chapter seeks to answer some of the questions.
6. Put up three large sheets of poster paper. Label one: *Developing Awareness*. Label the second: *Deepening Understanding*. Label the third: *Developing Conviction*. Ask for three volunteers to be recorders. They will write with felt-tip markers on the sheets the main comments as you lecture on the three sections.
• For your lecture on "Developing Awareness" show the Equipping Center module *The Priesthood of the Believer* and any books listed in chapter 8.
• During your lecture on "Deepening Understanding" have the group do personal learning activity 18. Discuss the answers.
• During your lecture on "Developing Conviction," call on the enlisted per-

sons to comment briefly on the books assigned to them.

7. Review briefly what has been written on the poster sheets.

8. Distribute worksheet 5. As you comment on the main points of the section "Becoming Involved in Ministry," ask members to fill in the worksheet.

9. When the worksheets have been completed, collect them. Give them to the pastor. Ask him to make plans to provide for needs implied on the worksheets.

10. Conclude the study with a two-fold prayer: (1) one of request that each participant would discover his/her spiritual gift and area of ministry and (2) one of dedication that each one would begin to minister.

Session 1

Introduction, Chapter 1—The People of God, Chapter 2—Motivation for Ministry

Session Goal: After completing this session, participants should have a better understanding of God's people as unique. Participants will be able to (1) explain the essence of the uniqueness of Christians; (2) compare Israel and new Israel; (3) summarize what the conversion experience is; (4) explain how the foundation for the motivation of ministry is found in the conversion experience; and (5) tell one specific action to give evidence of being a part of God's people.

Session 2

Chapter 3—The Ministry of the Laity, Chapter 4—The Nature of God's Mission and Ours

Session Goal: After completing this session, participants should have a better understanding of the ministry of the laity and the nature of God's mission/our mission. Participants will be able to (1) define the meaning of the priesthood of all believers; (2) explain the call to ministry of the laity; (3) identify the nature of God's mission; and (4) state a way to be involved personally in God's mission.

Session 3

Chapter 5—The Pastor as Equipper

Session Goal: After completing this session, participants should have a better understanding of the role of the pastor as equipper. Participants will be able to: (1) identify biblical material related to calling; (2) define the task of the pastor; and (3) describe some areas where equipping is necessary.

Session 4

Chapter 6—How Ministry May Be Expressed, Chapter 7—Gifted for Ministry

Session Goal: After completing this session, participants should have a better understanding of ways ministry may be expressed and giftedness. Participants will be able to: (1) describe how ministry may be expressed; (2) identify an aid for discovering spiritual gifts; and (3) identify ways to express spiritual gifts in ministry.

Session 5

Chapter 8—Where Do We Go From Here?

Session Goal: After completing this session, participants should have a better understanding of how the doctrine of the laity can be implemented. Participants will be able to: (1) identify an awareness, an understanding, and a conviction about involvement in ministry; and (2) make plans for personal and church implementation of laity involvement.

Visual Aid 1

ABRAHAM

ISAAC

JACOB

MOSES

Visual Aid 2

Outline Poster of Chapter 2
MOTIVATION FOR MINISTRY

I. God's Call in the Conversion Experience
   A. Limited understanding of the conversion experience
   B. Deeper view of the salvation relationship
   C. Not enough ministers

II. The Meaning of Faith
   A. Faith—fundamental part of being saved
   B. Exhortation rather than explanation
   C. Biblical passages on salvation
   D. Reexamination of conversion experience
      1. Salvation is gift
      2. The gift—is it conditional or unconditional?
      3. Understanding the condition
   E. Salvation—status/relationship
   F. Authentic faith

III. Our Response
   A. Faith that involves a personal relationship
      1. God as Creator and Father
      2. Divine mission of Father
      3. Ministers of the mission of reconciliation
      4. Gifted people
   B. Authentic faith

Visual Aid 3

144

EVERY CHRISTIAN IS A PRIEST.

GOD IS AT WORK APPROACHING THE BELIEVER.

THE BELIEVER HAS A RESPONSIBILITY TO SEEK OUT HIS/HER SPIRITUAL GIFT.

THE CHURCH HAS THE RESPONSIBILITY OF PROVIDING AN ADEQUATE PROGRAM FOR GIFT DISCOVERY.

THE CHURCH MUST AFFIRM OR NOT AFFIRM AN INDIVIDUAL BELIEVER'S CALL.

EVERY CHRISTIAN IS A MINISTER.

THE CALL TO SALVATION AND THE CALL TO MINISTRY ARE ONE AND THE SAME CALL.

THE PRIMARY RESPONSIBILITY FOR MINISTRY RESTS UPON THE SHOULDERS OF THE LAYPERSON.

Visual Aid 4

Outline Poster on
SOCIAL INVOLVEMENT

  I. Social involvement, a necessary aspect of God's eternal redemptive mission

 II. Objections to social involvement
    A. Fear of "the social gospel"
      1. View of being "nurtured" into the kingdom
      2. Identification of "liberal theology" and social involvement
    B. Other institutions than the church ministering to human needs

III. Social involvement, a necessary part of God's mission
    A. Persons—not dualistic
    B. Bible speaks of a person being a unity

TRUTHS BASED ON EPHESIANS 4

1. The means of equipping is the local body.

2. Every believer is a minister.

3. Believers must be equipped for ministry.

4. The purpose for equipping is to produce growth in the body of believers.

5. The pastor has the responsibility for providing the guidance for getting believers equipped.

Visual Aid 6

AREAS IN WHICH LAITY NEEDS TRAINING

Knowledge of the Bible

Knowledge of Doctrines

Knowledge of Church Functions

Knowledge of Church History

Knowledge of Missions

Knowledge of Christian Ethics

Skills in Witnessing

Skills in Teaching

Skills in Visiting

Skills in Counseling

Skills in Administering

Visual Aid 7

TRUE OR FALSE STATEMENTS

The church has not provided enough help to the laity for ministry in the family, in daily life and work, or in the political arena.

A focused ministry is a specific ministry, is a significant ministry, is a ministry to which one is called by God, is consciously self-chosen, and is a ministry for which one feels God has given him or her a gift.

Four major areas where a focused ministry may be found are: (1) through the structures of society; (2) through one's vocation; (3) through the needy areas of society; and (4) through the organizational life of the church.

Each Christian should be involved in only one major area of ministry.

The laity can express a Christian ministry only by assuming a leadership role in the church.

Visual Aid 8

SPIRITUAL GIFTS

(From 1 Cor. 12—14; Rom. 12:3-8; Eph. 4:11-12; 1 Pet. 4:10-11)

Leadership
Teaching
Knowledge
Wisdom
Prophecy
Spiritual Discernment
Exhortation
Shepherding
Faith
Evangelism
Apostleship
Miracles
Helps
Mercy
Giving
Healing
Tongues
Interpretation of Tongues

Visual Aid 9

Do not become
discouraged.

Have a dream.

Seek harmony.

Consider your leadership
style.

Visual Aid 10

Worksheet 1

1. Who is the new Israel? _____

_____

_____

2. To what is the new Israel called? _____

_____

_____

3. What is the essence of the uniqueness of God's people? ____

_____

_____

Assignment: Write below one specific action you will take to give evidence that you are a part of God's people (the new Israel). ____

_____

_____

_____

_____

_____

_____

_____

_____

Worksheet 2

Read Romans 3:23; Ephesians 2:3; and Romans 6:23.

1. How do you define sin? _____

_____

_____

2. Why does the world try to minimize sin? _____

_____

_____

_____

3. Why can man not save himself from sin? _____

_____

_____

_____

Read John 3:16; 2 Corinthians 5:19; 1 Peter 2:24; Mark 10:45; John 3:3; 2 Corinthians 5:17.

1. What does "believeth" mean in John 3:16? _____

_____

_____

2. What does "reconciling" mean in 2 Corinthians 5:19? _____

_____

_____

3. What does "be born again" mean in John 3:3? _____

_____

153

Worksheet 3

Complete the following statement.
I can be involved personally in God's mission

in my church life by _____

_____

_____

_____

in my home life by _____

_____

_____

_____

in my work life by _____

_____

_____

_____

in my social life by _____

_____

_____

in my political life by _____

_____

_____

_____

_____

Worksheet 4

As you read the section "Guidelines for Confirmation of One's Ministry," fill in the blanks in the statements below.

—The three guidelines used to confirm the focused ministry God has

for you are: (1) you will have a sense of _____; (2) you will

_____ _____ _____; and (3)

you cannot help but _____ _____ _____.

—The "ought-overflow tension" is _____

_____

_____

_____

_____.

—God's call and God's gift come together (mesh) at the point where

we _____ doing any _____ for

which we are _____.

—We may have a gift, but not do it particularly well because we have

not _____ _____ _____.

—It is possible that one's ministry may _____ _____

_____ _____ _____ throughout one's life.

Worksheet 5

Complete the following.

1. My answers to personal learning activity 18 tell me that my church _____

_____ .

2. I know what my spiritual gift is. _____ yes _____ no

   I know what my ministry is. _____ yes _____ no

3. I am willing to discover my gift and my ministry by (check as many as apply):
   _____ a. Studying *Discovering Your Spiritual Gifts*.
   _____ b. Studying the concept of call.
   _____ c. Studying a specific area of equipping in which I need help. (What area? _____)

4. I am willing to become a part of a mission group, become equipped, and be commissioned by my church. _____ yes
_____ no

5. I can minister in the marketplace by _____

_____

_____

_____ .

6. I would like for the church to take the following action to involve the laity in ministry:

_____

_____

_____ .

_____
(Name)

The Church Study Course

The Church Study Course is a Southern Baptist educational system consisting of short courses for adults and youth combined with a credit and recognition system. More than five hundred courses are available in twenty-three subject areas. Credit is awarded for each course completed. These credits may be applied to one or more of the more than one hundred diploma plans in the recognition system. Diplomas are available for most leadership positions, and general diplomas are available for all Christians. These diplomas certify that a person has completed from five to eight prescribed courses. Diploma requirements are given in the catalogs.

Complete details about the Church Study Course system, courses available, and diplomas offered may be found in a current copy of Church Study Course Catalog and in the study course section of Church Materials Catalog. Study course materials are available from Baptist Book Stores.

The Church Study Course system is sponsored by the Sunday School Board, the Woman's Missionary Union, and the Brotherhood Commission of the Southern Baptist Convention.

How to Request Credit for This Course
This book is the text for course 05045 in the subject area Baptist Doctrine. This course is designed for five hours of group study.

Requirements for Credit
Credit may be earned in two ways.

1. *Group study*. Read the book and attend group sessions. (If you are absent from one or more sessions, complete all of the personal learning activities for the material missed.)

2. *Individual study*. Read the book and complete all of the personal learning activities. (Written work should be submitted to an appropriate church leader.)

To Request Credit
A request for credit may be made on Form 725, Church Study Course Enrollment/Credit Request, and sent to the Awards Office, Sunday School Board, 127 Ninth Avenue, North, Nashville, TN 37234. The form on the following page may be used to request credit.

A record of awards will be maintained by the Awards Office. Twice each year copies will be sent to churches for distribution to members.

CHURCH STUDY COURSE
ENROLLMENT/CREDIT REQUEST (FORM-725)

INSTRUCTIONS:
1. Please PRINT or TYPE.
2. COURSE CREDIT REQUEST — Requirements must be met. Use exact title.
3. ENROLLMENT IN DIPLOMA PLANS — Enter selected diploma title to enroll.
4. For additional information see the Church Study Course Catalog.
5. Duplicate additional forms as needed. Free forms are available from the Awards Office and State Conventions.

PERSONAL CSC NUMBER (If Known)

TYPE OF REQUEST: (Check all that apply)

☐ Course Credit
☐ Enrollment in Diploma Plan

☐ Address Change
☐ Name Change
☐ Church Change

CHURCH

Church Name

Mailing Address

City, State, Zip Code

REQUEST FOR

DATE OF BIRTH ⬆ | Month | Day | Year

☐ Mr. ☐ Miss
☐ Mrs.

Name (First, Mi, Last)

Street, Route, or P.O. Box

City, State, Zip Code

COURSE CREDIT REQUEST

Course No	Use exact title
05045	1 The Doctrine of the Laity
Course No	Use exact title
	2
Course No	Use exact title
	3
Course No	Use exact title
	4
Course No	Use exact title
	5

ENROLLMENT IN DIPLOMA PLANS

If you have not previously indicated a diploma(s) you wish to earn, or you are beginning work on a new one(s), select and enter the diploma title from the current Church Study Course Catalog. Select one that relates to your leadership responsibility or interest. When all requirements have been met, the diploma will be automatically mailed to your church. No charge will be made for enrollment or diplomas

Title of diploma		Age group or area
1.		
Title of diploma		Age group or area
2.		

Signature of Pastor, Teacher, or Study Leader	Date

MAIL THIS REQUEST TO ➡

CHURCH STUDY COURSE AWARDS OFFICE
RESEARCH SERVICES DEPARTMENT
127 NINTH AVENUE, NORTH
NASHVILLE, TENNESSEE 37234

FORM-725 (Rev 7-83)